Thoughts to Inspire

Daily Messages for Young People

Edward P. Fiszer

ScarecrowEducation
Lanham, Maryland • Toronto • Oxford
2004

Published in the United States of America
by ScarecrowEducation
An imprint of the Rowman & Littlefield Publishing Group, Inc.
4501 Forbes Boulevard, Suite 200, Lanham, Maryland 20706
www.scarecroweducation.com

PO Box 317
Oxford
OX2 9RU, UK

Copyright © 2004 by Edward P. Fiszer

All rights reserved. No part of this publication may be reproduced, stored in a retrieval system, or transmitted in any form or by any means, electronic, mechanical, photocopying, recording, or otherwise, without the prior permission of the publisher.

British Library Cataloguing in Publication Information Available

Library of Congress Cataloging-in-Publication Data

Fiszer, Edward P. (Edward Peter), 1970–
 Thoughts to inspire : daily messages for young people / Edward P. Fiszer.
  p. cm.
 Includes index.
 ISBN 1-57886-124-1 (pbk. : alk. paper)
 1. Success—Juvenile literature. I. Title.
BJ1611.2.F56 2004
158.1—dc22

2004002485

Printed in the United States of America

∞™ The paper used in this publication meets the minimum requirements of American National Standard for Information Sciences—Permanence of Paper for Printed Library Materials, ANSI/NISO Z39.48-1992.
Manufactured in the United States of America.

Contents

Preface   v

Thoughts to Inspire   vii

Special Days   147

Subject Index   163
Author Index   165
About the Author   167

Preface

The power of positive thinking in connection with goals is the greatest concept not overtly taught to young people. This collection of passages is designed to remedy this problem. Through daily positive messages young people can be exposed to the idea that positive thoughts influence actions which in turn lead people toward their goals.

A negative environment is detrimental to future success. A young person overwhelmed by messages broadcasting that success is unattainable will believe what he or she hears. The positive must conquer the negative. The subconscious is a goal-seeking, problem-solving mechanism that works with the information it is fed. Stephen Covey mentions this concept in his book *The Seven Habits of Highly Effective People* (New York: Simon & Schuster, 1990). He and other experts recommend that goals and to-do lists be reviewed either before bed or early in the morning. This allows the subconscious to focus on the positive information it has recently been fed.

This collection is a teaching tool to be used by educators or family members. Possible applications are endless but a few suggestions include reading these passages aloud before bed to end the day with a positive message or each morning as an inspirational start of the day over the sound system to all classes or by a teacher to his or her class. I recommend these passages be reviewed by the reader with an eye to customize the message according to his or her experiences as well as the needs of the audience. Personalize the messages and use them as a springboard for further discussion. Whether as an educational leader or the caretaker of a child, a voice of inspiration can provide a memorable, lifelong impact on young minds.

How often do young people hear this sort of positive information? Success stories or thoughts about tenacity are sorely lacking in today's world. These passages are written with the intent to help educators and families combat the relentlessly negative messages young people are exposed to through various sources including the media. Negative self-talk is common in young people as well as adults and is deeply rooted in the environment in which they are raised. Such negative self-talk works against tenacity since it is inherently opposed to risk taking. School leaders and family members should associate themselves with positive thinking and stimulate positive morale, successful school involvement, and higher attendance. The encouragement of young people to determine and reach their goals will be felt and remembered.

THOUGHTS TO INSPIRE

Tenacity/Goal Setting

Vincent Van Gogh

Can you build a house by yourself in one day? You really couldn't. It's way too much work to accomplish in a short time. To build a house, you'd need to create the blueprints first to show how large the house should be and to help you figure out the materials you need in order to get started. Then you'd need to be able to work carefully and patiently to put every little piece in just the right place. Great things cannot happen quickly, without planning.

Artist Vincent Van Gogh wrote: "Great things are not done by impulse, but by a series of small things brought together."

Little by little you can move toward a large goal. Each day school provides you with practice to help build the skills you'll need later in life. You cannot learn it all in one day or in one year. You need to consistently apply yourself over time.

So today if you find something to be challenging, do your best because it is the small, difficult things you learn now that help you create a great future little by little.

Tenacity

Conrad Hilton

It's sometimes hard to keep going after you make a mistake. It's easy to feel angry and just want to quit. Someone who knew about working through problems and overcoming mistakes was the man who started the Hilton hotels, Conrad Hilton. From the time he purchased his first hotel in 1919 he had to keep working through any problems that came up and learn from his mistakes.

He said: "Achievement seems to be connected with action. Successful men and women keep moving. They make mistakes, but they don't quit."

The first Hilton Hotel opened in 1925 and today, because Conrad Hilton didn't quit, there are over 500 Hilton hotels around the world.

So today when things get difficult, don't give up. Learn to keep going and you will be successful.

Habits/Tenacity

Aesop

A habit is something you do repeatedly. Your habits shape who you are. People know you by the habits you have. If you always listen and follow directions, others know they can ask you questions because you know what is happening in the classroom. If you have the good habit of doing your homework as soon as you get home every day, you know how good it feels to play and watch television because you've taken care of your responsibilities. Your friends would be very surprised if you didn't turn in your homework. A habit is something you can develop every day.

The writer Aesop stated: "Little by little does the trick." Think of an area where you need to improve. If you need to memorize math facts, spend a few minutes every day practicing with flash cards. If you arrive at school late, make it a habit to leave your home earlier every day. If you don't exercise at all, you can do a little exercise every day and make it into a habit. Little by little, you can choose areas where you can improve and develop positive habits.

Listening

Ernest Hemingway

Ernest Hemingway wrote: "I like to listen. I have learned a great deal from listening carefully. Most people never listen."

You can learn so much by listening. Those who choose not to listen miss out. They don't learn as much and they're not prepared for what will happen next. One way to help you listen is to think about what you think will happen next and see if it happens. See if you can predict the answers to a particular activity you are doing in class. This kind of guessing game can make listening more fun than if you tell yourself you don't like to listen.

Tell yourself you are a great listener, that you want to learn more, and you really want to find out what will happen next.

Your Speech Reflects Your Character

Aristides

You talk about things that are important to you. If you talk about good things that are happening, you enjoy hearing about good things. If you are someone who complains a lot, you want to hear complaints—otherwise you would be talking about solutions to the problems rather than just letting people know how bad you think things are. Your words reflect your values and your character. You have a responsibility to others at school to make your school a great place. You should show your level of responsibility by talking about how to make things better, how you can help others, and that you think doing the right thing is important.

An ancient Greek philosopher named Aristides said: "As the character is, such is the speech."

What you talk about reflects who you are. So today show that you care about making good things happen by saying positive things to others.

Emotional Energy

Do you know how to maintain a high energy level? Rest recharges your physical, emotional, and mental batteries every night. Besides sleeping at night there are other things you can do to help yourself have more energy. Sleep helps you stay physically alert for you to exercise and do physical things in class.

You also have emotional energy. This kind of energy is easy to maintain during the day if you are positive. Negative people who get angry easily tire themselves out by being upset about things and telling others about problems.

Emotional energy is closely connected to the third kind, mental energy. Mental energy is used when you use your creativity. This may be to solve problems or write a report or book.

Instead of getting angry, you will have more energy if you look at a problem calmly, find a solution, and do what you need to do to make things better. When you get rid of your emotional energy by getting angry easily and staying angry, you will feel physically tired and not want to do your work.

So today, if you stay positive about what you are doing and do things to solve problems you are having rather than staying angry about them, you will have more mental, emotional, and physical energy to do your best in school.

Helping Others

Ralph Waldo Emerson

Ralph Waldo Emerson once wrote that no one "can sincerely try to help another without helping himself."

What does this mean? When you help someone, you show that you are caring, responsible, and are respectful of others. As you help someone you take things that you know and encourage or teach others. You know that as you help that person, you are building a friendship. By helping someone, usually that person will try and help you if there is a time when you might need help.

Helping others helps you because you will feel better about yourself since you used your time and energy in a positive way. Find ways to help others and you'll see that Emerson was right.

Goal Setting

Washington Irving

*W*ishing or hoping for something is not the same as working hard to accomplish goals. If you wish you knew your multiplication tables but didn't spend time practicing with flash cards or doing worksheets, your wish probably won't come true. If you make it your purpose or your goal to learn math facts, then you will think of ways to practice them at school and after school to make sure you do. After you put in the time and do the work, you'll accomplish your goal.

Washington Irving, who wrote *Rip Van Winkle* and *The Legend of Sleepy Hollow*, said: "Great minds have purposes, others have wishes."

So today consider what your purposes and goals are. Think of what you need to do for these things to happen and go to work on them. If you are only sitting there hoping and wishing for them to happen, they probably won't.

Choices/Actions Reflect Character

George Eliot

Your choices show who you are. The things you do and the things you say show the thoughts you have in your mind. If you are kind and friendly, you will do things that help others. You can shape what you are thinking by doing good things even if you don't feel like it. Once you start doing nice things for others you can put yourself in a better mood. It is hard to feel angry if you are doing something nice for someone else. Then the nice things we do stay with us throughout the day and help shape our thoughts.

Author George Eliot wrote: "Our deeds still travel with us from afar. And what we have been makes us what we are."

She is saying that we show what we are thinking through the things we do. So today show that you are a good citizen who is eager to help your teachers, friends, and others.

Learning

Carl Sagan

There are so many things everyone can learn. No one can know everything in a lifetime. Even people who read and study every day know that they have a lot to learn. You can learn to speak many languages, take up new hobbies like painting or sewing, or participate in sports. You should think of every day as a great new opportunity for you to learn something new—maybe your ideas will help you discover something incredibly new that the world has never seen before.

Carl Sagan once said: "Somewhere, something incredible is waiting to be known."

Remember that there are new things to be discovered by those who dare to be curious.

Try New Things

Vincent Van Gogh

Don't be afraid to try new things. If you don't try to learn new skills and figure out complex things, you won't have any fun. Your favorite author, musician, artist, or film star had to have the courage to try something new and amazing to get started in their career.

Artist Vincent Van Gogh asked: "What would life be if we had no courage to attempt anything?"

Have the courage to attempt great, new things. Be ready to live out your dreams by learning the skills you will need to do amazing, fun things with your life.

Exercise

Did you know that physically active children have fewer chronic health problems than kids who are not active? This means if you are not physically active you might not be as healthy as you could be. When you don't exercise much you might put on too much weight and your body will begin to feel tired all the time. When you feel tired you don't exercise as much and your body's organs don't work as hard to process the food you eat.

Exercise helps your body stay healthy and it also helps you think. If blood and oxygen are circulating throughout your body, your brain is better able to think and understand new ideas.

So at recess, lunch, and PE, as well as at home, exercise because it has many benefits. Whether you hike, sled, do push-ups or sit-ups, walk, play games, skate, ride a bicycle, dance, jump rope, or participate in organized sports, try to encourage your friends to participate with you. Exercise is a healthy habit you should keep for the rest of your life.

Practice

Anne Bronte

$\mathcal{D}$id you know that your skills and abilities get better through practice? Just like exercise makes your muscles stronger, the practice of math, reading, and writing make your abilities improve in these areas.

British author Anne Bronte wrote: "All our talents increase in the using, and every faculty, both good and bad, strengthens by exercise."

The people you choose to be with also will help you develop the good or bad habits that you practice. Choose your friends carefully and do your best in all assignments and you will increase your talents.

Talents

Oliver G. Wilson

*W*hat would happen if only people with great, amazing abilities got things done? What would everyone else be doing with their talents? Everyone at _____ has great talent in something and can use their talent to make a difference.

Oliver G. Wilson said: "Use what talents you have; the woods would have little music if no birds sang their song except those who sang best."

So today remember to use the skills you have to get great things done at school. You are probably not the best at everything but the things you do with your talents can make _____ a better place.

Improvement

Liz Ashe

What is one area where you can improve? If you had to choose one, would it be your writing, your behavior in class, or turning in your homework regularly? Choose a few things and work on putting a lot of effort into those areas.

Professional speaker Liz Ashe talks to people about making good choices in whatever career you choose. She says: "Don't try to be great at all things. Pick a few things to be good at and be the best you can."

It is hard to be really great in all areas all the time so start with a few areas where you know you need improvement. Write down in class or at home the areas where you really need to improve and this will help you focus. You won't be able to change the way you do things immediately but if you work on a few areas every day, you will make great improvement.

Opportunities

Ralph Waldo Emerson

Every day you have many opportunities to learn new things through the new opportunities your teacher creates for you in class. You have opportunities at recess and lunch to make new friends and do good things for others outside of your classroom. Opportunities to make good choices that will help others are all around you.

Ralph Waldo Emerson wrote: "The world is all gates, all opportunities, strings of tension waiting to be struck."

So today remember that the world is filled with gates that lead you to opportunities to do great things.

Citizenship

Edward E. Hale

The term citizenship means the duties, rights, conduct, and responsibilities of the citizen of a state. You are expected to do your share to make your school and community better. You should cooperate with others, stay informed, vote, be a good neighbor, obey laws and rules, respect authority, and protect the environment.

Author and clergyman Edward E. Hale wrote about how people can do something to make a difference. He said: "I am only one, but still I am one; I cannot do everything, but still I can do something; and because I cannot do everything I will not refuse to do the something that I can do."

A good citizen does not stop doing good things because others are not doing good things. Good citizens keep working to make their community better by remembering that their choices make a positive difference.

Problem Solving

Henry Ford

Henry Ford lived from 1863 to 1947. He founded the Ford Motor Company and knew a lot about how to get great things done. Henry Ford said: "Don't find a fault; find a remedy." A remedy is another word for a solution to a problem. If there is some type of problem around you it won't help to find fault or try and blame someone for the problem. Good citizens work on solutions to problems rather than talking about the problem and who is at fault.

At _____ find ways to solve problems so that you spend your time doing positive things and your focus remains on all the great projects your teachers carefully plan for you.

Environment

Sandra Day O'Connor

Every day we can make things better for others or make things worse. If all _____ students display great citizenship, the new students who enter our school will know that this is a school where people do good things for one another. If students make poor choices it is like they are damaging the environment, making our school unsafe. Since _____ students are only here for about ___ years, it is important that we keep our school a positive place for the new students who will join _____ in the years to come.

United States Supreme Court Justice Sandra Day O'Connor had a similar thought about how we should take care of our planet. She said: "As stewards of this planet, we need to make sure that we don't damage it. And if we can, we must leave it better than when we came."

Every day remember that we have a chance to make our environment the best it can be and that the choices we make can damage or improve our environment.

Opportunities/Choices

Peter Marshall

As you go through school you are given many opportunities to learn and grow. Some of those opportunities happen among the friends you make. As you make new friends remember that they can teach you positive or negative things. Since you are responsible for your own choices remember that you don't have to wait for your friends to tell you what to do or think—you can choose to do what is right even if others around you disagree.

Peter Marshall, an American clergyman, said: "Let us not be content to wait and see what will happen, but give us the determination to make the right things happen."

You can make the right things happen by making your own choices. Do what you know is right. Your choices can help others learn to make the right choices as well. Your good example can make _____ a wonderful, safe place for all students.

Positive Influences

Lance Armstrong Profile

The Tour de France is a bike race that happens each year. Only the best bicycle riders in the country can compete in a race that continues over 23 days and is 2,125 miles long. As of 2003, Lance Armstrong has won the Tour de France five years in a row. Lance Armstrong says he relies on his team to help him. His team is made up of nine bike riders who ride ahead of him to shield him from high winds that would make his ride even more difficult.

Since this sports hero couldn't win without great people around him, think about how he had to choose those people. He had to know their strengths and that they would encourage him to do what he needs to do. He wouldn't want lazy, negative people around him.

You should do the same when you are choosing your friends. Choose to be with people who do good things. The habits of others can make you a better person or lead you to make poor choices.

Reading

Rene Descartes

Rene Descartes is considered one of the most important thinkers to have ever lived. He lived from 1596 to 1650 and was a scientist, mathematician, and philosopher. He had a lot to say about the importance of books.

He said: "The reading of all good books is indeed like a conversation with the noblest men of past centuries . . . in which they reveal to us none but the best of their thoughts."

You can read the greatest thoughts of others in books. Even though the authors may have lived hundreds of years ago, you can still learn a lot from them. It is like having a conversation with these people. So take advantage of the wide variety of books you have available at the library at school, the public library, or at any bookstores you visit.

Positive Thinking

Arnold H. Glasow

We can always count on things changing in some way. Whether we experience a problem or something wonderful, we can count on that experience changing in some way.

Arnold H. Glasow said: "Nothing lasts forever, not even troubles."

Problems can seem to take a long time to finally get resolved. It always helps to be confident that solutions will present themselves and that better things are about to happily surprise us.

Talents/Boldness

Thomas Wolfe

Author Thomas Wolfe says: "If a [person] has talent and cannot use it, he has failed."

Any person who has the abilities to do great things but chooses not to make use of those abilities will not be very successful. It is like this in school. If you do not show your teachers what you can do, you will not receive good grades on your report cards. Your teachers have to see the proof of your talents in your work in order to give you good grades.

So make sure to show all that you can do. Don't hide any of the talents and abilities that are in you. If you show people what you can do, you will be more likely to do great things with your talents in your future.

Success/Tenacity

Thomas Henry Huxley

Did you ever notice that each step of a ladder is used to get somewhere else? Each of those steps is called a rung and each rung allows you to go higher and higher. They are not very comfortable to rest on if you are trying to get to the roof of a house or someplace else you couldn't reach without a ladder. Scientist and writer Thomas Henry Huxley noticed how rungs of ladders only hold people for a short time on their way up.

He said: "The rung of a ladder was never meant to rest upon, but only to hold a man's foot long enough to enable him to put the other somewhat higher."

You should think of each day at school as the rung of a ladder. Each day is not meant to be wasted but to help you learn more and more to prepare you for the next grade. As we go through the school year, show your teachers you understand how important the lessons they carefully prepare are. Show that you appreciate their hard work by following directions closely.

Positive Thinking

Alan of Lille

$\mathcal{D}$id you ever notice that when bad things happen, good things can happen almost immediately? When something makes us sad or upset, we need to remember that a variety of things will happen to every person—good and bad. Remembering that good things will happen to us can make the bad things that happen easier. People have known this for centuries.

In fact, a writer known as Alan of Lille who lived from 1128 to 1202, wrote: "After the greatest of clouds, sun."

Storm clouds can come through, bringing rain for long periods of time, but the sun eventually comes through and brightens the day. Just as we don't know how long the clouds will stay with us, we do know that the sun will shine again. This is something to remember when bad things happen—just like stormy clouds, the bad things will go away and good things will happen very soon.

Reading

Chinese Proverb

Did you ever notice how being in a garden can make you feel better? It might be that we see and smell beautiful plants and flowers and breathe fresh air while we are outside. We also may become aware of how pretty things can be in an environment different from what we are used to at school or at home.

Books are a lot like gardens because they can transport us into different environments. Books can make us notice different things about the world.

There is a Chinese proverb that compares gardens to books that says: "A book is like a garden carried in a pocket."

So today look forward to reading a book if you feel bored at home or want to enjoy a different place. Books can take you to amazing, wonderful places.

Tenacity

Angie Matsoff Profile

There are people with impairments in this world who continue to do great things. They don't give up just because they have extra problems that most other people do not have. In fact, they are great examples to others of what is possible if people persevere in accomplishing goals. Some people have visual impairments that make things like driving a car or riding a bike almost impossible. Their vision is so poor that they might only be able to see very blurry shapes so if they were to go jogging or swimming they could bump into something and get seriously hurt.

A woman named Angie Matsoff didn't let this type of disability stop her. With the help of her husband, Angie Matsoff participates in marathons and triathlons. How does she do it? How did she compete without hurting herself when her vision is so blurry she cannot see details, just shapes? During bike rides of over 100 miles, she rides a tandem bike with her husband—that's a bike that has two seats for two people to pedal. For the 2.4 mile swim part of a triathlon, she trains for months to swim in a straight line with other swimmers helping her stay on course. During long runs her peripheral vision allows her to see the edge of the pavement and spectators along the course which helps her not miss any turns during the race. Despite her visual impairment she earned a university degree in health and fitness and owns a gym where she works as a personal trainer.

This is a great example of accomplishing a great deal by not giving up—even if you have a disability that makes reaching your goal even more difficult.

(*Source: Runner's World,* July 2003)

Challenges/Confidence

Alonzo Newton Benn

As you start each day remember that you have the chance to show what you can do. Through your actions you show what matters to you and what doesn't. You show how you respond to challenges. Every day school is about challenging your abilities to help you grow. The way you think about these new assignments will help you do well.

Alonzo Newton Benn is credited with saying: "Meet the sunrise with confidence."

Each day is a new opportunity to grow. Be confident that you will do your best and you will do better than if you arrived at school unwilling to try your hardest.

Health/Drinking Water

How important is it to drink water? Here are some essential reasons:

- Water is a major component of our blood, which transports all the other nutrients to our cells. It also transports toxins and metabolic waste to be removed from our cells.
- Water helps carry waste products out of the body.
- Water in sweat dissipates heat through the skin, which helps our body to maintain internal body temperature.
- Water plays a vital role in the transmission of our nervous system's nerve impulses.
- Water helps to dissolve and digest nutrients.
- Water is involved in the biochemical reactions in our body to produce and release energy.
- Water in fluids surrounds our joints, providing lubrication and mobility.

So, now that we can see how important water is to our body, here are a few more practical things:

- Lack of enough water is the #1 cause of physical fatigue, especially during exercise, so let's start drinking before exercise.
- We are dehydrated before we feel thirsty, so we should not wait until we are thirsty to drink. Some other signals that we may be dehydrated are headaches, chills, and mental fatigue.
- Every time we drink coffee, soda, diet soda, or alcohol, we increase our water need.
- Exercise and warm weather will increase our water need.

So today make sure to drink enough water.

Fears/Confidence

Eleanor Roosevelt

You become stronger and more confident when you try new things. People who are too afraid to try something new let their fears get in the way of new experiences. Their fears keep them from growing.

Eleanor Roosevelt once said: "You gain strength, courage, and confidence by every experience in which you really stop to look fear in the face."

So today at _____ , don't be afraid to try something new. Remember that you become stronger and more confident whenever you face your fears.

Show Appreciation

Vietnamese Proverb

*D*o you say thank you to others? There are many opportunities every day to show gratitude for what you have or the kindness others show you. When someone offers to help you with a project or opens a door for you, you should say thank you to let the person know you appreciate their help.

There are other times when we can simply think about how lucky we are to have good things around us. We should appreciate our teachers, our school, our families, our friends, and many others.

There is a Vietnamese saying that relates to the food we eat: "When eating a fruit, think of the person who planted the tree."

There are many people who do good things who deserve appreciation. If you have a chance to thank someone, let them know they are appreciated. If you show appreciation and think about all the good things in your life, you will be a happier person.

Make a Difference

Sir Thomas Fowell Buxton

Sir Thomas Fowell Buxton lived in England in the late 1700s and early 1800s. He worked against the practice of slavery and to make changes in the prisons in England.

He said: "The longer I live, the more I am certain that the great difference between the great and insignificant is energy—invincible determination—a purpose once fixed and then death or victory."

Throughout his life he had to face many people who were against his ideas so he'd really know about determination and using your energy to do something very important.

Today, show that you know your energy can be used for important things at school like completing your work and helping others. If you do good things with your energy, you will make the world a better place.

New Ideas

Thomas Watson

The world needs great, new, surprising ideas. If people didn't have amazing ideas that seemed impossible, we wouldn't have things we use every day like telephones, cars, or computers. A company called IBM started over one hundred years ago by making punch cards that would help the census, a time when the government counts the number of people living in the United States. Since that time they've been looking at different ways to help businesses get their work done.

In 1943 the chairman of IBM, Thomas Watson was discussing the future of computers and said: "I think there is a world market for maybe five computers."

He thought the world wouldn't need many computers because the idea was so new. He died in 1956 and would be very surprised to see how this new idea of making computers for adults and children to use would be a great thing. This shows how new ideas can be so strange that people may not believe they are necessary or possible. But without new ideas we would never have new ways of doing things.

So if you have a great idea or hear someone sharing a new idea, encourage them to find a way to make it happen. Write down your ideas and draw pictures of how your ideas can help the world. If you do, you may be starting something new that people will be grateful for in the future.

Goal Setting/Obstacles

Sydney Smith

Clergyman Sydney Smith was called the wittiest, wisest man in England during his time. He lived from 1771 to 1845. He did a lot of thinking about how people reach their goals.

He said: "Obstacles are those frightful things you see when you take your eyes off your goals."

If you think an assignment is too hard, think about how you know you need to keep trying to get it finished. If you tell yourself it is impossible to finish, you are seeing the obstacles to finishing it. Instead really focus, ask another student or your teacher for help—but DO NOT sit there and think about how you cannot do it.

Keep the goal of finishing and learning in mind and you will get your work done. Then once you're finished you'll feel proud of yourself because you accomplished your goal.

Work Hard

Sophocles

Trying your hardest to learn or get your work done is the greatest thing you can do to be successful in school or after your graduate from school and get a job. People who don't work hard are usually hoping they get a good grade or have good things happen to them. Hope won't help you get a good grade. This has been true for centuries.

In fact, twenty-five centuries ago, a Greek writer named Sophocles wrote: "Fortune cannot aid those who do nothing."

He was saying that fortune, luck, or hope will not help the person who chooses not to work. Great things happen to people who try their best. So today, try your hardest on whatever assignments you are given and show that you know the harder you try at something, the more successful you will become.

Confidence

Franklin D. Roosevelt

How can you generate feelings of confidence about the things you do? Franklin D. Roosevelt, the thirty-second president of the United States, said it has to do with honesty and how well you do what you need to do.

He said: "Confidence . . . thrives only on honesty, on honor, on the sacredness of obligations, on faithful protection, and on unselfish performance. Without them, it cannot live."

He is saying that if you are dishonest and do not make sure to do the very best you can, you will not be confident about what you are doing. The dictionary defines confidence as faith or belief that one will act in a right, proper, or effective way.

Today make sure to do things in a right, proper, and effective way by being honest and trying your best.

Healthy Habits

How does our body fight disease and what can you do to help keep your body healthy?

If a germ passes through our skin, nose, or throat and mouth and gets into our blood stream, there are special cells in our blood that fight germs. There are two types of fighting cells in our body, white blood cells and antibodies. White blood cells eat harmful germs. Antibodies attack specific germs that they have been in contact with before. For example, if you have had the chicken pox before your body has created antibodies to the virus that causes chicken pox. If you are exposed to the chicken pox again these antibodies will attack that virus. This is why you can only get the chicken pox once. How do we prevent the spread of germs to other people and keep ourselves from getting sick?

Hand washing—keep your hands clean because the germs that are on your hands can be passed on to whatever food you will put in your mouth when you eat OR will get on the things or people you touch—spreading the germs to others.

Covering our mouths when we cough or sneeze—don't help spread germs by forgetting to cover your mouth when you cough or sneeze.

Wash our dishes before we use them again—cooked food should go on clean plates before you eat.

Keep food that needs to be cold in the refrigerator or else it can go bad, making people who eat it very sick. These healthy habits as well as eating lots of fruits and vegetables, getting plenty of rest, and drinking lots of water will help keep you and others healthy.

Excellence/Hard Work

Pearl Buck

How can you experience joy when you are working? Would you think that someone who has written over seventy books and won the Nobel and Pulitzer prizes for literature would know something about enjoying your work?

Pearl Buck lived from 1892 to 1973 and won many awards for her many books. About work, she said: "The secret of joy in work is contained in one word—excellence. To know how to do something well is to enjoy it."

To become excellent you must practice and work hard. No one is excellent at something they are trying for the first time. The difficult part is sticking with new things until they become easy. Once they become easy you will feel the joy that excellence brings because you will have mastered the skills your teachers have you practice.

Time Management/Listening

To do well in school you need to manage your time well. You need to do what is most important according to your teacher and not waste your time. Being a good listener helps you manage your time.

If you are not a good listener, you might end up doing things that are not important. You can really only do one thing very well at a time. When you are in the middle of something, really focus until you are finished. If you cannot focus, you'll forget important details and not get everything you need to accomplish done very well.

So today make sure to be a good listener and make good use of your time. If you follow directions well, you will receive good grades.

Intentions

Robert C. Edwards

It is easier to become successful if you are trying to do good things. It is harder to be successful if you want to do things that will not help others.

Your intentions are the thoughts that motivate you. They describe why you do the things you do. If you want to be helpful, your intentions are to be kind to someone else. You might be making someone feel better when they are sick or helping your teacher clean the room when you are finished with your work. Good intentions lead to good actions that will help you feel happy when you do good things. You know that you are helping someone else and that makes you feel good inside. If you are always selfish and angry when you don't get your way, it is likely that you are unhappy most of the time.

Robert C. Edwards, a former president of Clemson University in South Carolina, said this about intentions: "The path to success is paved with good intentions that were carried out."

He is saying that if you have good intentions to help others and act on them, you will be successful. So when you think about what you'd like to be when you are older, think of what good intentions go along with what you want to be. If you want to be a teacher, you might think about all the students you will help when you are older. If you want to be a doctor, you might think of all the people you can help feel better. If you would like to be a reporter, think of how important it is to interview people or to write about what is happening in the world so others can read about great events.

If you have good intentions with the things you do, you are very likely to be successful.

Thoughts/Dreams/Goals

Michael Korda

Everything you do starts with a thought. You have to think of doing something before you do it. You cannot really say you don't know why you did something because at some point you it seemed to be an okay thing to do and the thought led you to action. Your thoughts lead you to make good choices or bad choices. Your thoughts lead you to achieve great things you might never have considered before. This means if you set an incredible goal, somewhere in your mind the thought starts working on how it can become reality. Dream big dreams, think about the many things you want to be when you are older. Don't just stick to one idea like being a doctor or a soccer player—think about how you can be both of those things.

Michael Korda, who for many years was the editor in chief of a publishing company called Simon & Schuster, said: "The more you can dream, the more you can do."

If you do not dream, you won't have any great ideas going on in the back of your mind about your future. At home keep a list of all the different things you'd like to be and do. If you write them down, it'll help you really think about your dreams.

Since everything starts with a thought, fill your mind with the things you'd like to have happen to you in your future and you will make them come true.

Positive Thinking

*D*on't focus on what others are doing wrong and how to get them in trouble. When you watch for someone else to make a mistake you are wasting your time and your mental energy.

Think good, positive thoughts that focus on your work. If you spend your time paying attention to directions and the lessons your teachers prepare for you, you will have less work and studying to do at home. If you are watching for mistakes others make, you are wasting your time.

So today put your time to good use by paying attention to how you can improve your learning and not to mistakes others make.

Tolerance

Tolerance is a word used to describe how people should feel and behave regarding those from different cultures or having different beliefs. If someone is different from you because they are from another country, speak a different language, or belong to a different religion, then there are things you can learn from that person. If you are only around people exactly like you, you wouldn't learn as much about the world compared to time spent with people with different beliefs.

The United States is famous for having all different types of people living here peacefully. It is not strange for people from many different countries to live on the same street and to shop in the same stores. In other countries this does not happen. We are very fortunate to be able to learn from one another and should enjoy this opportunity.

So today remember that _____ is a wonderful, unique place where people from a variety of countries, religions, and cultures are welcomed and deserving of respect.

Self-Control/Thoughts

Ralph Waldo Emerson

You control what thoughts you have. Since you control what you think, you control what you do about your thoughts. Even if others are trying to give you bad ideas, you are the only one who can choose to keep those thoughts in your mind.

Ralph Waldo Emerson was a famous writer and philosopher who lived from 1803 to 1882. "Your own mind is a sacred enclosure into which nothing harmful can enter except by your promotion."

He means that you can close your mind to any harmful, bad thoughts. It's your choice.

To say that someone else told you to do something shows you allowed someone's bad thoughts to stay in your mind and influence your actions. Instead always keep good, positive thoughts in your mind. If you protect what you are thinking and keep good ideas in mind, you will do great, helpful things.

Tolerance/Respect for Others

*Y*our family's culture is part of who you are. It is like your hair color, and height. It is part of you. No one can do anything about it, it is what it is. One of the reasons you go to school is to learn about others. You learn how to solve problems with others and you learn how others think and do things. Learning how to get along with other people is an important skill that will help you do well in life.

Since schools are places where people need to learn to get along with others, they are places where respect is necessary. You need to show respect for others just like you would like to be respected. If anyone at _____ thinks they do not need to show respect for others, they are wrong.

Anyone who says something insulting about another person's religion or culture is trying to hurt that person. If you hear someone say something mean and disrespectful about another person, tell them to stop. People who are from different places, learn differently and think differently, help make our school a wonderful place. Show that you are a caring person who respects the differences in others.

Problem Solving

Victor Hugo

Victor Hugo was a famous French author who wrote many great books including *Les Miserables*. He once described big problems to be like thick ropes.

He said: "The greatest blunders, like the thickest ropes, are often compounded of a multitude of strands. Take the rope apart, separate the small threads that compose it, and you can break them one by one [and you will think] 'That is all there was!' But twist them all together and you have something tremendous."

When you copy someone else who is doing something wrong, you make the problem bigger. If you know someone has made a mistake and you don't tell them, you make the problem bigger. But if you know you can help by solving a problem, help solve it right away.

Even if others are telling you not to help, do what you know is right and help solve a problem from the beginning.

Exercise

A study was conducted in the spring of 2001 by the California Department of Education. Approximately one million students were given reading, math, and fitness exams. The students were in fifth, seventh, and ninth grades. In all grades the students who did better in fitness areas such as strength, flexibility, and aerobic fitness, which is how far and how fast they run, did far better in the reading and math areas.

This shows that students who exercise more do better in school. We know this is true because exercise helps blood and oxygen circulate to your brain and helps you think better, feel more alert and awake, and allows you to focus longer than if you did not exercise.

So today, make sure to exercise. It will help you do better in school.

(*Source*: *Runner's World*, April 2003, p. 19)

Work Habits

$\mathcal{D}$id you know that your work habits can indicate how well you will do in your job when you finish with school? Your work habits in school involve understanding directions, making yourself do your work, and finding good things to do with your time. If you develop a reputation for speed, dependability, and quality work, you will immediately stand out from other students who choose to waste their time and not finish their assignments. It works the same way when you have a job in the future. The people who get the best jobs and are given the most responsibilities are the people who understand what is the most important thing to do with their time right now and work on what is most important until they have finished.

Don't be the type of person who is known for not getting work done. If you spend all your work time talking and not paying attention to directions, you won't be able to get everything done and the parts you do finish probably won't be of the best quality.

If you finish the most important work first and find extra things to do when you are finished, you're already training yourself to use your time wisely and be the best at whatever job you choose to have in your future.

Persistence

Hank Aaron

Persistence makes you successful. If you persist in doing your work to the best of your ability, every time, even when things get difficult, you will improve. It is too easy to give up when something is difficult. If you give up, you'll never get better.

Hank Aaron was a baseball player who hit 755 home runs over his twenty-three-year career. He also established twelve other major league records in addition to his home run record. He was asked what his secret was. He said: "My motto was always to keep swinging. Whether I was in a slump or feeling badly or having trouble off the field, the only thing to do was keep swinging."

Even when he was having problems or feeling badly, he kept trying. Being persistent made him a great success. So today, think of an area where you need to improve and be persistent when it gets difficult. You'll experience success if you are persistent.

Trustworthiness

Henry David Thoreau

Trustworthiness can mean many things. It can mean telling the truth and being reliable. It can also mean something bigger—it can mean standing up for your beliefs and living your life by your principles. If you believe something with all your heart, you will always stick by what you believe and not do things that are contrary to that belief. A trustworthy person who believes it is incredibly important to listen to his or her teachers will not disobey their teacher because they live by the principle that following a teacher's instructions is important. If you are someone who believes that caring for the environment is important, you won't litter, but instead you'll pick up after yourself and make sure you leave your school and your home neat and clean.

Henry David Thoreau was an American writer and philosopher who said: "Live your beliefs and you can turn the world around."

He is saying that people who make choices based on what they believe will influence what others do. Over time you can influence the world by what you do. Whether you are a good example or not, others notice what you do and learn from it.

So when you hear the word trustworthy remember that it also has to do with the choices you make because your choices have to do with what you think is important.

Caring

Jane Addams

What does it mean to be caring? The word caring describes someone who is kind and shows concern for others. A caring person gives his or her time to help others without thinking about what can be gained from it. A caring person thinks about how other people feel.

A good example of a person who is caring was Jane Addams, the first woman to receive the Nobel Peace Prize.

In 1889, when she was twenty-nine, Jane and her friend, Ellen G. Starr leased a large home built by Charles Hull at the corner of Halsted and Polk Streets. The two friends moved in with the purpose of making Chicago a better place to live by helping others.

Together they convinced other people to help them care for sick people, poor people, and children. They started kindergarten classes and afterschool programs and by the second year it was open, people called it the Hull House. They helped two thousand people every week. There were night classes for adults who needed help learning to read. Over time Jane Addams became a member of the Chicago School Board and helped lead the way for women to have the right to vote. She even accepted a position as garbage inspector at one point. She did all she could to help others.

So today, think of ways that you can show others that you are caring. You can make the world a better place.

Persistence

When you work on something, do your best until it is done. Be persistent in your work. Do not allow yourself to be distracted by other things going on in your classroom. Think about how you can do the best job you possibly can until your work is complete.

This can be very difficult because it's sometimes fun to start thinking about other things. But the best part is that the more you discipline yourself to persist on a major task, the more you like and respect yourself. You feel better about yourself when you get your work done and you know it's the best you can do.

And the more you respect yourself and feel better about yourself, the easier it is for you to discipline yourself to persist even more on harder tasks and get more done throughout the day.

So today, be persistent in your work, don't let others distract you so you can finish your assignments and feel good about the work you've done. If you do this every day, you will need to study less at home because you're paying closer attention in class.

Water/Brain

$\mathcal{D}$id you know that getting enough water to your brain is important? It is especially important for children whose brains are growing and developing every day. Eric Jensen in *Teaching with the Brain in Mind* (Alexandria, Va.: Association for Supervision and Curriculum Development, 1998) tells us that dehydration or not getting enough water leads to fatigue and learning problems in children. Some children will feel much more awake after a few days of having regular water intake. This means when you are thirsty—drink water. Your body is telling you what you need.

Drinking water assists your body in using the food you have eaten in the right way, helping the lungs, heart, and blood vessels while energizing the brain and body.

Think of a living sponge. A sponge cannot do a great job unless it is wet. Without water your brain cannot do it's job very well. So at recess and lunch, get a drink of water and drink more water at home to help your brain do the best job it can.

Truth

Aldous Huxley

This school is a wonderful place because of the hard working teachers, staff, and students. It's a place where people know learning is important and a place where everyone should feel safe. Whether in the classroom or on the playground, you are able to help keep others safe by following directions and telling the truth. If you are asked to do something or go somewhere by someone who works here, you need to do it and show that you want this school to be safe by following directions. This is really important if there is a drill happening or if there is a problem at school. Every time a student tells the truth, they make _____ a better school. Don't ever think that not telling the truth will help a problem. If you do not help the school by saying exactly what happened when a problem comes up, it's like you are hoping the problem will go away by ignoring it. Ignoring the truth won't change what has happened.

A writer named Aldous Huxley once wrote: "Facts do not cease to exist because they are ignored."

When you ignore or don't tell the truth about a problem, you help it become a bigger problem. So today, make sure to help make this school a wonderful place by telling the truth and following directions.

Responsibility/Choices

Elisabeth Kubler-Ross

Who is responsible for what you do? You are the only one who is ultimately responsible. If someone is a bad example, you do not need to copy what they do. If someone tells you to do something you know is wrong, you make your own choice whether you should do it or not.

Elisabeth Kubler-Ross was a psychiatrist who lived and worked in the United States and Switzerland. Her books have been translated into more than twenty-five languages. She wrote: "I believe that we are solely responsible for our choices. And we have to accept the consequences of every deed, word, and thought throughout our lifetime."

When you make a choice there is a consequence of that choice. The more good choices you make, the more good consequences you will enjoy from those good choices. So today be a good example to others by showing you know you are responsible for your choices and are ready for the consequences that come with those choices.

Self-Control/Paying Attention

You control the things you do. If you change the things you do, you can make your results better or worse. If you start studying and working more, your grades will improve. If you start studying and working less, your grades will get worse.

Small differences in your performance can lead to large differences in your results.

Notice what successful students do and imitate them. By paying closer attention in class and taking better notes, you might have to study less at home. If you talk less when the teacher is talking, you'll probably understand more and need to take less unfinished work home.

You can make a big difference in your learning by paying closer attention to what your teacher says and finishing as much work as possible during the school day.

Exercise

*W*hy is it important to exercise?

Exercise helps blood and oxygen travel throughout your body. This helps your brain think clearer than it would if you didn't exercise. People who don't exercise are usually a lot more tired than people who do exercise. Your body is made up of muscles and organs that need movement to feel their best—if the body doesn't move very much, the muscles begin to get weak and therefore have less energy.

Your body puts on extra weight when you don't exercise. Carrying extra weight on your body is like carrying a backpack filled with huge books on your back all day long. Excess weight tires you out. It makes your heart, lungs, and muscles work harder than they need to.

So today make sure you exercise. If you do, you'll feel better and think better than if you don't exercise.

Trustworthiness

ARE YOU A TRUSTWORTHY PERSON?

True or False?

- Do you keep your promises at home and at school?
- Are you loyal to others unless they tell you to do something you know is wrong?
- Are you reliable? Do you do what you say you will do?
- Are you honest?
- When people tell you personal things that you know shouldn't be repeated, do you keep those things a secret or do you tell others these things?
- Do you have integrity or if someone suggests you do something that you know is wrong, do you consider doing it?

Think about your answers. If you are trustworthy you show it by what you choose to do. If you are not trustworthy, start acting like a trustworthy person by making choices consistent with trustworthiness.

Success/Failure

B. C. Forbes

To do amazing things you have to try to accomplish amazing things. Don't be afraid to try to stretch your abilities and believe you can do something amazing.

B. C. Forbes, the founder of Forbes magazine, said: "The men who have done big things are those who were not afraid to attempt big things, who were not afraid to risk failure in order to gain success."

So today, as you're doing a writing assignment, try to do a better job than you've ever done. Keep in mind that you can do amazing work if you're not afraid to try your hardest.

Problem Solving/Responsibility

Chinese Proverb

There is a Chinese proverb that says: "Better to light a candle than to curse the darkness." Darkness can mean a problem exists. It does not help to get really angry. When you are getting angry, a smart thing to do is to give yourself a moment to calm down and think about what is happening and why. Think about other people who are involved and what they may be thinking and feeling.

By stopping and thinking, you are able to be responsible—to control your response to what is happening. If you're not sure how you can help solve the problem, talk to an adult.

When you stop and think about a problem and look for a way to help the situation, it is like you are lighting a candle in the darkness rather than getting upset at the darkness and doing nothing about it.

Potential

James T. McKay

James T. McKay once wrote: "No matter what the level of your ability, you have more potential than you can ever develop in a lifetime."

Never think you've learned all that you can learn. You're never finished. There is so much to know and do in this world that there's never any reason to stop.

If you are at the top of your ability, you can still learn new things. You can get better at whatever you choose to focus on. Your report card is a great indicator of what areas you should focus on. Use this tool to figure out what your needs are. Spend all your time in class trying your hardest to get better and you will.

Your potential never ends. If you give up when things get difficult, you will never know how great you can be.

Energy

$\mathcal{D}$o you know how to maintain a high energy level? Rest recharges your physical, emotional, and mental batteries every night. Besides sleeping at night there are other things you can do to help yourself have more energy. Sleep helps you stay physically alert for you to exercise and do physical things during the day.

You also have emotional energy. This kind of energy is easy to maintain during the day if you are positive. Negative people who get angry easily tire themselves out by being upset about things and telling others about problems.

Emotional energy is closely connected to the third kind, mental energy. Mental energy is used when you use your creativity. This may be to solve problems or write a report or book.

Instead of getting angry, you will have more energy if you look at a problem calmly, find a solution, and do what you need to do to make things better. When you get rid of your emotional energy by getting angry easily and staying angry, you will feel physically tired and not want to do your work.

So today, if you stay positive about what you are doing and do things to solve problems you are having rather than staying angry about them, you will have more mental, emotional, and physical energy to do your best in school.

Choose Your Attitude

Viktor Frankl

𝒴ou have the power to choose what you will think and do. You choose to pay attention in class or you choose to daydream. You can choose to get angry at something or you can stop and think about what has happened and take action to help solve the problem.

Viktor Frankl was a medical doctor who was imprisoned in several concentration camps during World War II. While he was in prison he saw that even when people face horrible things, they still have the right to choose what they think about. He believed that if you have something meaningful to think about and look forward to, you will be okay when things get difficult.

He wrote: "The last of the human freedoms [is] to choose one's attitude in any given set of circumstances, to choose one's own way."

The power to choose one's attitude and thoughts is our greatest freedom. Today choose to make _____ a wonderful place to be by learning all that you can.

Teaching Others

Would you be a good student today if you were never taught how to read? Did your parents and teachers give up when you were learning or did they give you many chances to learn the alphabet and all the sounds letters make? Did they help you learn to write or did they give up because it may have taken a lot of practice to start forming letters into words? Maybe they took their time because they know that people need time in order to acquire great skills. People need to be given chances before they can make amazing things happen. Someone has to give someone else a chance by helping them.

So today just as someone helped you learn to read and write by being patient with you, look for a way to help someone else. You can make a big difference for someone else by giving them a chance to learn something new or help them do something better than they have ever done before.

Actions/Choices

John Ruskin

John Ruskin was a poet, artist, and scientist who lived in England during the 1800s. He said: "What we think or what we believe is, in the end, of little consequence. The only thing of consequence is what we do."

All that matters is what you actually get up and do, not thoughts you have. You can think it's important to be good to others but it doesn't matter unless you show your thoughts through your actions. The same is true about your grades. You are given grades based on what you do. You can understand everything and be the smartest person in the world but if you do not show your teacher what you know, you will not get good grades. Show all that you know by giving answers aloud in class or in writing in your assignments.

Show what you are thinking on the playground by making good choices. You can think and believe that people should follow the rules but if you don't show what you are thinking through your actions, your thoughts and beliefs don't really matter.

So today at _____ , show what you believe and know through the work that you do in class and the choices you make.

Goal Setting

Julieanne Louise Krone

In 1993 Julieanne Louise Krone, thirty, became the first woman anywhere in the world to win a top-ranked thoroughbred horse race.

Julie was raised on a farm in Michigan. She was only nine when her mother bought her a horse and enrolled her in the Pony Club of America. Soon Julie was riding in horse shows.

At fourteen, Julie watched on television as Steve Cauthen won the Belmont Stakes. She turned to her mother and said: "I'm going to be a jockey." Julie and her mother went to Churchill Downs where both got jobs walking racehorses.

Julie knew what she wanted to do and she looked for ways to accomplish her goals.

Julieann Krone once said: "A lot of incredible things can happen when people are given chances."

So today, if you hear about what someone else wants to be when they are older, give them a chance by encouraging their dreams and share your dreams with them. Decide what you want to be and make a plan to achieve your goals. You can do amazing things.

Making Mistakes

*A*re you afraid to make mistakes? It's not fun to be wrong but don't be afraid of making mistakes either. The more mistakes you make, the more you are trying to learn something that you don't already know. To learn how to walk, you have to fall as you get better and better. To learn to ride a bike, did you ever lose your balance? Of course you did. When you started reading, did you need help? Everyone needed help learning to read.

We all make mistakes as we learn. If you are too afraid to raise you hand and take a chance on being wrong, you won't learn as much.

So today, try your hardest and don't be afraid to make a mistake.

Goal Setting

Brian Tracy

An author named Brian Tracy writes a lot about goal setting. He once wrote: "No one is better than you—some people are just better developed and more knowledgeable in certain areas."

Someone who exercises every day is going to be more fit than someone who does not exercise at all. It is not that the person who exercises is a better person, they just make different choices about what they should do with their time and become better developed physically.

Someone who reads every day exercises their mind so they become more knowledgeable about the subject they are interested in. These people become more knowledgeable and are able to think about things differently from people who do not read and study.

If you think of someone you admire, think about what the person does with his or her time. If you want to have the same abilities as that other person, force yourself to spend time doing the things that person does and you will end up with similar abilities if you spend your time doing the same types of things to the best of your ability.

Attitude/Positive Thoughts

Colleen C. Barrett

Did you know that your attitude determines how you feel about what you are doing?

Colleen C. Barrett, the president of Southwest Airlines, once said: "Work is either fun or drudgery. It depends on your attitude. I like fun."

Drudgery means something really boring and horrible. If you think something will be horrible, it will seem horrible. Your attitude becomes part of what you experience.

In class, if you think your work is fun, it will feel like you're having fun.

So today, send yourself positive messages to make you feel good about what you are doing. If you look forward to it, you will likely do better work.

Time Management

Vilfredo Pareto

Did you know that for most people 80 percent of the value of what they do is made up of 20 percent of what they do? This is called the 80/20 rule or the Pareto Principle, named after Italian economist Vilfredo Pareto. He noticed that people spend the majority of their time doing things that are less important. His theory is that 20 percent of your tasks are much more important than the rest of your tasks and therefore should be done first.

Think about what happens when you get home. The most important things to do are your homework and maybe some chores around the house. That's your 20 percent. What happens with the rest of the time or the other 80 percent of your time at home? Some students watch television or play outside and delay doing their homework and chores until much later.

People who use their time wisely will do the most important things first because they decide what few things they should do that matter the most—then they leave the rest for later. By doing the most important things first, you will feel better about yourself. The most important things may take the most time to accomplish but they are worth it. They matter the most among all the things you have to do so don't procrastinate—get started and don't let anything distract you from getting your homework and chores done first.

Choices/Actions

$\mathcal{D}$id you know you are remembered for what you do? Everything you do and the way you do things helps others get to know who you are. People think of you as neat or messy, helpful or just helpful once in a while, or as someone who either makes good choices or is learning to make good choices.

Show who you are by what you do. The best part of this is that even if you've acted a certain way all year, you can change the things you do. If you didn't make good choices or didn't do good work, you have the power to change what you do and people will notice.

So today show people the kind of person you really want to be by the things you do. Be a kind person who helps others. Be someone who gets important work done well. This reputation will make you one of the many valuable and respected people at _____.

Do More Than You Are Required

Charles Kendall Adams

*Y*ou have to do more than is required of you to be a great success. Do more than you are asked. If your teacher asks you to read at least five pages—why stop at five? Keep going. Do more. If your parents ask you to clean your room—clean it and find some other way to help. Do more than you are asked.

Historian and author Charles Kendall Adams wrote about successful people. He said: "No one ever attains very eminent success by simply doing what is required of him; it is the amount and excellence of what is over and above the required that determines the greatness of ultimate distinction."

Doing more than you are required to do makes you great. This is one of the reasons why _____ is a great school. Your teachers do more than they are required to do to teach your class what they need to know. It takes a lot of planning and a lot of time to grade all the work students do. They don't do it all at school—they take it home and spend extra time doing it because they want to be successful with their students. Be like your teachers and do more than is required—if you do, you'll be much more successful.

Brain/Healthy Eating

What you do with your time and what you eat affect your health. Your brain and the rest of your body need a variety of foods to stay healthy. You should be eating fruits, vegetables, and some type of protein such as those found in nuts, meat, poultry, or fish each day. Your brain and body need these foods filled with different vitamins to keep you healthy and ready to learn. You will have more energy and get sick less if you eat a variety of these healthy foods. Potato chips, soft drinks, and candy are fine as occasional treats, but when they're eaten regularly, they can cause your body to gain weight and slow down. Your brain then hears messages that it is too tired to really focus because your body has to work harder to digest foods that aren't healthy.

Just as your body receives messages from the food you eat, your level of activity teaches the brain what is important to you. If you watch more than one hour of television each day, your body is probably not getting enough exercise. When your body does not get much exercise, you don't receive as much oxygen and blood circulating to keep your energy level high and to fight off the germs that would love for you to just sit around and let them make you sick.

So don't teach your body it is okay to just sit and watch television, make sure to exercise and eat vitamin rich foods to stay happy, healthy, and energetic.

Learn from Mistakes

Henry Ford

It is really important to keep experiencing new things. The more you try, the more you learn.

Car maker Henry Ford once said: "Life is a series of experiences, each one of which makes us bigger.... For the world was built to develop character, and we must learn that the setbacks and griefs we endure help us in our marching onward."

Even if we have problems, we learn from mistakes and that helps us develop as people. We keep moving forward and are less likely to make those same mistakes again because we are constantly learning and experiencing.

Your experiences help make you into a bigger, better person. Don't be afraid to make a mistake. Just make sure you learn from your mistakes as you keep trying new things.

Be Positive

*Y*ou can make your classroom better than it ever has been and you can feel better about yourself while it is happening. You can do this by being positive.

Positive emotions give you energy, while negative emotions deplete your energy. When you are excited and happy about being at school and spending time with your teacher and classmates, you sparkle with energy and enthusiasm. When you are angry or upset about something, or negative for any reason, you feel tired and frustrated.

So today, don't let anyone be negative around you. Look for the positives, encourage others by making good choices, and you will help make _____ a wonderful place to be.

Tenacity

Abraham Lincoln

Our sixteenth president, Abraham Lincoln, once said: "Always bear in mind that your own resolution to succeed is more important than any other one thing." This means that if you have decided to put all your effort into doing something very, very well, then that is what matters. It doesn't matter if someone else tells you not to do it. It doesn't matter if the people around you are not doing the same thing.

Deciding that you will be successful is very important. Decide what you want to be when you are older and link your grades to how successful you will be later. What you do now impacts how successful you will be later. Reading, writing, and math will come up in your life later whether you want to be a doctor, auto mechanic, or open a restaurant. You will need to be able to read new information, use math skills to keep track of how much money you make, and communicate with others through writing.

Your teachers are here to help you build your skills so that you will be successful in the future. The really important thing for you to do is decide what you want to be successful in and then think about how your reading, writing, and math skills will help you become a success.

Effort

Dwight D. Eisenhower

Is it hard to always do your best? It can be difficult because when you try new things, you will make mistakes and sometimes you will see others making bad choices or trying to tell us not to do what's right.

Our thirty-fourth president, Dwight D. Eisenhower, said: "No man can always be right. So the struggle is to do one's best, to keep the brain and conscience clear, never be swayed by unworthy motives or inconsequential reasons, but to strive to unearth the basic factors involved, then do one's duty."

He is saying we need to think about doing the right thing and the reasons why we should do the right thing. This can be hard because we may see others making bad choices or we might make a mistake once in a while.

So today remember do your best to make the world a better place by doing your best to follow the rules and show respect for one another.

Anger Management

Abraham Lincoln

When someone gets angry in class or on the playground and wants to have their way, why does that person need to raise his or her voice? Sometimes people think the louder they become, the more right they will be. If someone is out during a game and they yell that they are going to stay in, that doesn't mean they are correct. The rules are there to keep people doing what is right. Getting angry or using force to get your way does not make you right in what you are doing.

Our sixteenth president, Abraham Lincoln said: "Let us have faith that right makes might; and in that faith let us to the end dare to do our duty as we understand it." He is saying that doing what is right makes a person strong and mighty. Don't believe people should have their way just because they try and force other people to let them do something that is wrong. The person who uses force and anger is usually the person who is wrong. Might does not make right.

Instead, follow the rules and be around people who want to do what is right. Your example will show others that doing the right thing makes a person mighty.

Positive Thoughts

Frank Crane

Dr. Frank Crane lived from 1861 to 1928. He used to write a lot about how people think. He said: "Our best friends and our worst enemies are our own thoughts. A thought can do more good than a doctor or a banker or a faithful friend. It can also do more harm than a brick."

What do you think about all day? If you think about things you don't have or mistakes you have made, you are doing harm to yourself. Your mind becomes full of problems you have had and is not free to focus on the good things that will happen today.

So today think about all the ways you can help your class be a great class. Try your hardest to get all your work done. Think about how much smarter you are becoming and how fun it is to help others. These types of thoughts will help you focus on good choices.

Learning

Abraham Maslow

If you don't learn anything, you are really taking a step backwards. You are not putting any new information into your head and you're not changing the way you do things. Learning means you grow because you change something about yourself, even if it's just some thoughts that you have.

Abraham Maslow said: "You will either step forward into growth or you will step back into safety."

Don't worry about making mistakes as you grow and learn. When you try something new you are moving forward and growing. It is when you don't try, just to be safe, that you don't move forward.

Individual Greatness

Everyone has greatness within them. Everyone in your class right now has something about them that is very special. Sometimes that means you do very well in a particular area. You might be great in reading and writing but not so good when it comes to PE. One student may do well in math because he or she can see the numbers on the page and do the problems but things he or she hears in class may not be easy for that person to comprehend.

Don't make the mistake of thinking that students who may not do incredibly well in every area may not have greatness in them. Sometimes a person's greatness is visible much later in life in ways you wouldn't expect. The people in your room will do great things with their lives. What you should spend time doing is trying your best in class and helping anyone that you can help.

By helping others, you share your greatness and build friendships with people who will do amazing things in the years to come.

Tenacity

Michael Jordan

*D*o you work hard every day? Is it a habit with you or do you only really try on some days instead of every day?

Michael Jordan has always consistently practiced to be the great basketball player that he is. He said: "Success isn't something you chase. It is something you have to put forth the effort for constantly; then maybe it'll come when you least expect it."

He is saying you need to spend time consistently working and improving. Then before you know it, you will be amazingly successful.

Learning

Arie de Geus

Every day at _____ you are given assignments, projects, and tests that give you chances to exercise your brain. These carefully planned tasks are there to help you learn more every day. As you graduate from high school and college and start to work full time, you will be able to have great jobs if you learn quickly. If you get a job and show that you cannot learn from what is happening around you, the company will want to have someone else do the job.

Arie de Geus worked for a big company called Royal Dutch/Shell and through the biggest advantage a person can have in getting a great job is "the ability to learn faster."

So today at _____ use all the opportunities you are given to learn and pay close attention. By following directions and learning new things all the time, you will have great opportunities to work for exciting companies.

Reading/Learning

Jane Hamilton

Jane Hamilton, an author who lives in Wisconsin, says this about books: "It is books that are a key to the wide world; if you can't do anything else, read all that you can."

You can learn so much about different people, places, and ideas by reading. Books are often translated from other languages so ideas from other parts of the world can be understood in other countries. This means a book you write about something that happened to you can be translated for students on other continents.

By reading all that you can you will understand new things about the world. By doing your best to become a better writer, you can add incredible ideas to the literature of the world.

Thinking/Dreaming

Vincent Van Gogh

$\mathcal{V}$an Gogh was a great artist who lived from 1853 to 1890. He was very poor throughout his life. People did not buy many of his paintings like they do today. His brother Theo used to help him when he needed help. There are many books about the letters Vincent would write to his brother Theo about what he was thinking and feeling as he painted.

Vincent once said: "I dream my painting, and then I paint my dream."

Before you do anything, you usually have at least a small idea of what you are going to do. Vincent Van Gogh had an image in mind before he started painting. The writing you do at _____ is very similar. Think about what the finished product will be before you start. This could mean while you're brainstorming notes, maybe using concept organizers a lot of classes use, you should get your ideas together and shape what your writing will look like before you begin.

Then when you get started on the actual writing, you'll have a clear focus in mind and create a wonderful version—just like Vincent Van Gogh.

Anger Management

What can you do when you're angry? Give yourself a time-out. Count to ten. Remind yourself that you have choices. If you are angry and do something mean to someone else—be ready to pull a card in class, miss recess, or even be sent to the office because there are consequences for bad choices. When you know you can choose not to push someone else or not say mean things, don't do it. Stop and think, are you making a good choice or a bad choice? Think about how you'd feel if someone was mean to you.

What are the good consequences of taking your own time-out and making good choices? The good consequences include: knowing you can make good things happen for yourself, knowing you are a good example for others, knowing you won't get in trouble with your school or your parents, and knowing that your friends will want to be with you because you're not going to do mean, crazy things to them.

So today at _____, if you're getting angry, take a time-out and think about the consequences of what you could choose to do.

Goal Setting

Alexander Graham Bell

Once you accomplish something great, there's no reason to stop and feel like you've finished. If you have mastered your multiplication tables, make sure you understand division. When you really understand one thing, figure out what else you should study. Keep going. It is a lot of fun to set goals and see them through successfully. It is even more fun to start working toward brand new goals because you feel good about yourself and you feel like there are exciting new things to work on.

One of the world's great inventors, Alexander Graham Bell, never allowed himself to stop learning and experimenting. He said: "The achievement of one goal should be the starting point of another."

As soon as Alexander Graham Bell was satisfied with what he was working on, he didn't stop setting goals. He kept working and discovering new and amazing things.

So today as you learn new ideas and practice your skills, remember that the world is filled with amazing new goals you can achieve. Once you accomplish one goal, get started on your next one. Always have lots of great things you'd like to accomplish and you will likely find ways to achieve them.

Failure/Success

Reggie Jackson

Reggie Jackson was one of the greatest baseball players ever to play the game. He was nicknamed Mr. October because he used to regularly hit homeruns for the Yankees if they made it to the World Series in October. To hit homeruns he used to sometimes strike out. He would strike out because he was trying. If he didn't take a chance on missing the ball, he would never hit a homerun. This was his way of overcoming failure.

He once said: "I feel that the most important requirement in success is learning to overcome failure. You must learn to tolerate it, but never accept it."

Reggie Jackson showed others how to be successful because he kept telling himself to keep trying until he was a success.

Today keep in mind that you will sometimes fail in order to become a great success. The key is to keep trying your hardest because you will eventually succeed.

Trustworthiness

Trustworthiness is a very important character trait. When you trust someone, you can rely on that person because he or she is responsible. That person has shown you that their word will come true. Trustworthy people do not lie to others. You can be confident that a trustworthy person will do their best.

How can you show you are trustworthy? A few ways could include being responsible and honest when doing your work in class and when on the playground. If your teacher asks you to do something, you will do it and your teacher can be confident that you will follow his or her exact directions. You can show you are trustworthy by always telling the truth, even if that means you or your friends could get in trouble.

Today at _____ , think of ways to show your teacher that you are trustworthy.

Brain/Rest/Learning

People from every part of the world, eagles that fly high in the sky, hippos in the jungle—they all need sleep! Sleep is as important as the food you need to eat and the air you need to breath. Did you know that people can survive longer without food than they can without sleep?

Sleep is vital for giving your body a rest from what you did during the day and the chance for it to prepare for the next day. It's like giving your body a short vacation. Sleep also gives your brain a chance to sort all the information you learned at school and from your experiences outside of school. Researchers who study the brain aren't exactly sure what kinds of organizing your brain does while you sleep, but they think that sleep may be the time when the brain sorts and stores information, replaces chemicals that were used up, and solves problems. After a good rest, you are better able to handle new problems and challenges.

So if you really want to be ready for school—don't stay up too late. Your brain will be glad to get the rest it needs to learn all that it possibly can.

Vision

What part of your body lets you read the back of a candy wrapper, look in the newspaper to see which movies are playing at our local theatre, and see a handball about to strike you in the head? What part lets you cry and makes tears to protect itself? What part has muscles that adjust automatically whenever you need to focus on things that are close up or far away? If you guessed the eye, you're right!

They are hard workers. In fact, your eyes are at work from the time you wake up in the morning to the second you close them to go to sleep. They take in information about the world around you—how things move, how things are shaped, what color things are, and more. Then they process the information and send it somewhere really important—your brain. Your eyes enable your mind to know what's going on.

Inner Beauty/Judgment

Michelangelo

Have you heard the expression "Don't judge a book by it's cover"?

The cover of a book may have a picture or a design you don't like but that doesn't mean you won't enjoy the story.

It's important to remember that there is a lot we don't know but can find out. We can find out what type of story is in a book by reading it. You can find out a lot about other people you don't know by being friendly and asking them questions to get to know them.

Michelangelo, a famous artist, said that inside every block of stone or marble dwells a beautiful statue. The block may not look like anything special but the sculptor just needs to remove the extra material on the outside to reveal the work of art within.

So today at _____ , remember that people and books can have many wonderful surprises in them so be ready to learn from books and people you may not have considered special.

Mistakes/Success/Failure

Albert Einstein

Is it okay to make a mistake? Of course it is. Although it can be a little scary to try something new, making mistakes is a way to help you get better because you notice when you get something wrong and fix it so you can get it right next time. If you don't try—you won't make a mistake but you also won't learn anything new.

The great scientist Albert Einstein said: "Anyone who has never made a mistake has never tried anything new." By trying new things you will learn an amazing number of things. Don't be afraid to make a mistake as long as you learn from them so that you are constantly improving.

Tenacity

Janeen Steel

According to an article in the Los Angeles Times, May 22, 2002, Janeen Steel graduated from UCLA law school and founded the Learning Rights Project at the Western Law Center for Disability Rights located at Loyola Law School. She helps students who are having difficulty at school make sure they get the help they need. She knows that some students have learning difficulties and need extra help.

Why would someone as smart as she is care about students with learning disabilities? Janeen Steel has dyslexia. This disability affected her ability to read and write and made school so hard that she dropped out of high school because it was so hard for her to pass her classes. BUT she kept trying and enrolled at Long Beach City College where a writing professor suspected she had dyslexia because the professors daughter had the same condition. That professor gave Janeen Steel the help she needed. Now Janeen Steel is helping others and loves what she does. Why is she a success? She didn't give up and someone else helped her when she needed it.

Today at _____ , find one area where you will not give up even when things get difficult and find a way to help someone else. If you do these things it will be a great day you will remember.

Choices/Anger

Lao-tzu

Have you ever seen children being mean to other children on the playground? It's easy to be mean to other people when you are angry. One thing to remember is that if you are mean to someone else, you are angry inside. The harder thing to do is control your emotions and understand why you feel the way you do.

A long time ago, an Asian philosopher named Lao-tzu said: "He who conquers others is strong; he who conquers himself is mighty."

It's easier to conquer others by being mean. It's harder to control yourself, figure out why you feel the way you do, and make yourself do the right things. If you make sure you make good choices that show you care about others, you are a stronger person than others who do mean things to other people.

Tenacity

Henry Ward Beecher

Part of getting really good at something is practice. When you start off at something new that you really would like to try, it's usually very difficult. If you're learning a sport like tennis or golf, it may seem difficult at first but you feel yourself getting better with practice. It's easy to be disappointed and to stop. The secret is not to give up. If you let a big disappointment stop you, you'll never get to be a great success. Sometimes a huge success can surprise you right after you've been a part of a failure.

Henry Ward Beecher, a great speaker who lived in the 1800s, said: "One's best success comes after their greatest disappointments."

So today at _____ remember that if you don't do well on a test or something goes wrong, keep working at it because a great success can come after a big disappointment.

Challenge/Success/Failure

Colin Powell

Secretary of State Colin Powell said: "There are no secrets to success. It is the result of preparation, hard work, and learning from failure."

Your preparation comes from paying attention in class, following directions, doing all your homework, studying for tests, working with others to solve problems, and so many other things planned for you to do at school. These actions lead you to success because they are difficult. If it seems too easy for you, you might not be learning as much as you could. It could be that you need to try harder, more challenging assignments. You can do this whether you are at school or on vacation. Look for challenging things to read at home or in the bookstore or library. If you challenge yourself and make a few mistakes, learn from your mistakes.

Learning from mistakes will help you become more successful since you will probably not make those same mistakes again.

Positive Thoughts

What should you do when you have a problem? If you're worried about something, think of the solution to the problem and talk to adults about how the problem can be solved. If you are faced with a difficulty do not think over and over about how you don't like the situation. Don't waste your time worrying and telling yourself that the problem will continue and continue.

Solutions are positive thoughts, whereas problems are negative thoughts. The instant that you begin thinking in terms of solutions, you become a positive and constructive person. Then talk to adults at school who can help solve the problem. If you don't do anything about the problem, it is like you are keeping it a secret and that will not help it go away. Tell the adults at school about a problem you are having and work with the adult on the solution.

If you focus on positive thoughts you will feel better because you are doing something positive rather than worrying about it.

Goal Setting

Samantha Riley

Samantha Riley is an Olympic swimmer from Australia. She started training with a coach to be a world champion swimmer when she was seven years old. She started training with a goal in mind even though she had severe problems with asthma. But this problem didn't stop her. She kept training and was able to compete in the Olympic games several times as well as other world champion competitions.

Samantha Riley said: "The most important thing to do is set goals. Training is a waste of time if you don't have goals."

Even if you are only seven years old and have a condition like asthma, you should be setting goals and figuring out what you want to do. If you haven't written down any goals at home, think about what you want to do. Consider what training or studying you will really need. List all these things in a journal at home. Write about what you want to be and why you believe it will make you happy.

If you write these things down and read over your notes regularly, you will probably find a way to meet your goals in the future.

Learning/Curiosity

Don Herold

*D*on Herold was an author who lived from 1889 to 1966. People enjoyed reading his ideas in *Reader's Digest* and other publications. He once wrote: "The brighter you are, the more you have to learn."

This means that the more you study, the more you understand how much there is to know about the world. People who read all the time are the ones who want to learn more. Anyone who sits around bored all day and thinks they have nothing to do or nothing to learn is someone who doesn't know a lot of things about the world.

As you get smarter, the more you want to know. It's good to be curious about things—it will make you want to know even more.

Reading

Jim Rohn

What kinds of books do you like? Mysteries? Funny books? History? Science? Do you ever think about how much you learn when you pick up a book? A lot of people read to find out about things. People who choose not to read are the ones who learn less.

An author named Jim Rohn says something interesting about books: "The book you don't read won't help [you]."

There could be one great book that helps you figure out what you want to be when you're older or how to solve a problem you are having. Remember that the next book you start reading could be the one that helps you the most.

Choices

Martin Luther King Jr.

What should you do when someone is a bad example?

Be a good example.

When someone you know is yelling at someone else or not doing their work or using bad language, remind them of what they should be doing.

DO NOT COPY THEM.

Dr. Martin Luther King Jr. said: "Darkness cannot drive out darkness; only light can do that. Hate cannot drive out hate; only love can do that. Hate multiplies hate, violence multiplies violence, and toughness multiplies toughness in a descending spiral of destruction. . . . The chain reaction of evil—hate begetting hate, wars producing more wars—must be broken, or we shall be plunged into the dark abyss of annihilation."

When you copy someone doing wrong, you create more badness in the world. Remember what Dr. King is saying and drive out anything bad from _____ by doing what is right.

Positive Thoughts/Contribution

Mahatma Gandhi

When bad things happen, it can seem like the people doing bad things have won. It seems like they have power and are getting what they want while other people suffer.

Mahatma Gandhi was someone who saw bad things happen but told people instead they should be a good example.

When he was sad because of bad things happening, he said: "[When I despair,] I remember that all through history the way of truth and love has always won. There have been tyrants and murderers and for a time they seem invincible, but in the end, they always fall—think of it, always."

Those who do bad things are not loved and do not make the world a better place. If something bad happens remember what Gandhi was saying, the way of truth and love or the good people who do good things for others are the ones who win.

Today do something good for someone else and help make _____ a great place.

Family/Show Appreciation

Alexander Graham Bell

Many years ago a speech therapist worked tirelessly to invent a machine that would allow deaf people to "hear" by making sound waves visible—this way the person could read what was being said. Unfortunately, the machine failed to achieve its purpose, but it was not altogether useless—that machine became the telephone. The man who was trying to invent that machine to help deaf people was Alexander Graham Bell. He never would have kept working so energetically on that machine if he didn't feel deeply that he should help the lives of the deaf.

Alexander Graham Bell was smart and encouraged to do great things by his mother and his wife. Both of these women were deaf. Alexander was committed to helping the people who were important in his life.

Think of ways you can help people important to you. What can you do for your family that shows them you appreciate their help? Find ways to help and show them how much you care.

Knowledge/Goal Setting

Linda Greenlaw

One of the few women involved in the commercial fishing industry, Linda Greenlaw has fished for swordfish, lobster, crab, halibut, and all sorts of other fish. She graduated from Colby College in Maine, and her first book is called *The Hungry Ocean*.

She is great at what she does, even though she has stories of how dangerous her job can be and how difficult it can be to find the fish she is looking for. Think of how much she needs to know in order to guide her ship through storms and travel all over the world.

She says: "What I do is called 'fishing.' If it was easy, we would refer to it as 'catching,' and there would be a lot more people doing it."

Think about what you want to be when you're older. Then figure out what you'll need to know to be the best at that particular job. Start reading about people who have that job now, talk to people who can help you learn about the training you will need. Then work to be the best in your chosen profession.

Positive Thinking

Kurt Vonnegut

Kurt Vonnegut once wrote: "We are what we pretend to be, so we must be careful what we pretend to be."

What do you think that means? If you do the things helpful people do, you will be a helpful person. If you do things mean people do, you will be a mean person. Even if you always do nice things but start to act like you are mean—you will become mean. The author Kurt Vonnegut was reminding people that we need to choose who we really are and what we act like. If you act like a great student and you listen and do all the work you can, you will become a great student. But some people tell themselves they cannot be successful or that others don't like them and it turns out that they are right. If you think positively about something and do positive things, then good things will happen.

Even if you haven't done well in a particular subject at school, tell yourself that you can do well, start to act like you do well in that subject all the time and do the things that people who are good in that subject do, and it is likely that you will be doing better than you used to in a subject you always thought was difficult.

Hard Work/Success

Theodore Roosevelt

*I*s what you're doing valuable? Doing something worthwhile makes a big difference. Many people like to work hard.

One of our country's presidents, Theodore Roosevelt, said: "Far and away the best prize that life offers is the chance to work hard at work worth doing."

All the different lessons your teacher prepares for you are helping you build your skills to prepare you for the jobs you will have in the future.

Working hard is the best prize in life. Think of the work you will do today at _____ as work that will help you have a great future.

Reading

Charlie Jones

Author Charlie Jones says: "You will be the same person in five years except for the people you meet and the books you read."

He is saying that your friends can change you—they can make you better or worse than you are. Books can change you—they can give you great ideas and lead you to think and do amazing things. Read all that you can instead of watching television and playing video games. If you read on your own every day for at least one hour, you will develop the habit of reading that will help you become smarter and smarter. Most adults don't read for an hour every night even though they should instead of watching television.

Are your friends telling you to do good things or bad things? What are you telling your friends they should do? Are you a good influence? Are you helping your friends do good things? Think of ways you can help others play fair on the playground and do good things in class. If you see others who are doing something wrong, maybe show them through your example what they should be doing in class instead of waiting for your teacher to tell them.

Constant Improvement

Nancy Thayer

Author Nancy Thayer says: "It's never too late—in fiction or in life—to revise."

When you are writing you need to be ready to edit you work and make changes. Your first copy is usually not your best. Be ready to make it better. Great authors make sure to look at their work again and again. Great writers make their writing better by reading it over and thinking about how it sounds, if the words are spelled correctly, if they can think of better ways to say the things they are trying to say.

It's never too late to make your writing better. REALLY listen when your teachers talk to you about writing because they will tell you secrets of how to improve. Even if you think it's finally finished, there are always ways to improve.

Just like in life—stop and think about the things you do, and you can always change what you're doing to help make the world a better place. Even if you think you're doing all that you can, you can revise what you're doing to make things better for others.

Tenacity/Success

Thomas Edison

*D*id you ever notice that people who don't get good grades don't like to study? They let their minds wander or just don't do their work. You need to make sure that you finish your work and do the things that will make you successful.

A great inventor who knew how important it is to try new things and keep working even if you're tired was Thomas Edison. He said: "The successful person makes a habit of doing what the failing person doesn't like to do."

So today make sure you do the things that hard workers do. Be a good example to those around you and show that your habits are the habits of successful people.

Brain/Depression

Mark Twain

What should you do if you are feeling sad?

A famous writer named Mark Twain said: "The best way to cheer yourself up is to cheer everybody else up."

If you ever feel sad the best way to feel better is to do something nice for someone else. When you do something good the brain releases endorphins, a chemical that makes you feel good and positive. When you do nice things for others and even when you exercise, your brain releases this chemical that makes you feel better.

PLUS when you do something nice for others, you make their day a better one too. So even if you are not feeling sad, do something nice for someone at _____ today.

Quality

Howard Newton

$\mathcal{D}$o your best work. Don't worry about being the first one who finishes.

Howard Newton said: "People forget how fast you did a job—but they remember how well you did it."

Whether it's writing or math or any other assignment, doing your best job means thinking carefully about what you need to do, reading all the directions, and reviewing what you've done to make corrections.

Don't think it's important to be the first one done—it's more important to do your very best.

Brain/Positive Messages

Margo Adair

$\mathcal{D}$id you know that your brain sends messages to your body all the time? Your brain tells your body what to do. You first have a thought, then you say or do something.

Author Margo Adair says: "At every moment, our bodies are continually responding to the messages from our minds."

So what messages is your mind giving your body? Send your body positive messages. Tell yourself to listen during class and do the best job you can all day, every day. Don't tell yourself that the assignment is too hard. If you send the message that you cannot do something, your body will believe it. Tell yourself to try and you will find yourself improving in everything you try to do.

Age Is Irrelevant/Success at Any Age

George Eliot

$\mathcal{D}$on't stop thinking of possibilities. If you think you want to be a doctor, teacher, lawyer, architect, actor, author, or any other thing you'd like to be, write it down somewhere and list all the people who can help you and all the things you should do to get ready.

George Eliot was an author in the 1800s who said: "It is never too late to be what you might have been."

She means you can get started on something great no matter how old you are. All you have to do is decide what you want to be, figure out what you need to do, then get started. It's never too late.

Health/Drinking Milk

*W*hy should you drink milk? It helps you develop strong bones because of the calcium and vitamin D it contains. A study was conducted by researchers who wanted to see how children who don't drink milk are different from those who drink milk regularly. Fifty children who had avoided milk between the ages of one to about six were compared with two hundred habitual milk consumers in the same age group in New Zealand. It was found that the milk-avoiders were not only shorter in height, but had worse bone health and much higher rates of bone fractures. While getting enough calcium is important throughout life, there's no time when it's more critical than in the developing years, when the bones are still growing.

Once you get to a certain age, you cannot develop new bone material, you can only prevent losing it by making sure you get lots of calcium.

So try to drink milk to help your bones develop. If you cannot drink milk, your doctor might tell you to take calcium and vitamin D to make sure your body gets what it needs to develop in the best way possible.

Focus

*W*hy do experienced animal trainers walk into a lion's cage with a stool in their hands? It tames a lion better than anything. The trainer holds the stool with the legs extended so the lion sees all four legs at once. Why does this work so well to keep the lion calm?

The lion tries to focus on all four legs at once and it can't. The lion is paralyzed. The lion prefers to focus on one thing at a time.

People work the same way. If you have too many things on your mind, it's hard to get anything done. Focus on one thing at a time. When there's an assignment from your teacher in front of you, focus on what you need to do right now. Don't think about other things. If your mind drifts to other ideas, you won't be doing quality work because you're like the paralyzed lion who tries to focus on too many things at once.

Do Extra/Read and Study More

Do you want to be a good student? One of the ways to make sure you are a good student is to do all that you need to do in class every day. Finish your work and pay attention.

Do you want to be a great student? Spend time outside of class doing extra reading and thinking. Make extra projects based on something you learned in class. Ask your teacher what you will be learning about next week and read ahead when you are at home. Go to the library to learn more about whatever you are doing in science or social studies. This is especially true when you are off track—your brain is like a muscle and needs to have exercise even when you are on vacation.

You are only in school about six hours every day. Spend time learning outside of class and you will be a great student. The more you read and study on your own, the easier it is to learn new things when you are at school and the more you will want to learn.

Opportunity

Dave Weinbaum

An opportunity is a chance. It means you can do something you may not have expected. It is usually something new or different.

At school your teacher presents you with a window of opportunity. Throughout the year you have specifically prepared assignments to help you to learn and grow. These are opportunities for you to enhance your skills.

It is like you are looking through a window at the well-prepared student your teacher believes you are. But you have to open the window by doing your work and studying. If you don't do your work and don't pay attention in class, you leave that window closed.

Dave Weinbaum, a famous businessman, says: "A window of opportunity won't open itself." He is saying you need to do something to make good things happen.

Your teacher can create all the great lessons for you but YOU need to do the work. Show your teacher that you want to learn with every assignment he or she gives you today.

Tenacity

Thomas Edison

Thomas Edison invented 1,093 different things. He was granted at least one patent every year for sixty-five consecutive years—this means the U.S. patent office recognized at least one new invention he created every year for sixty-five years. It took him ten thousand tries before he successfully created the first incandescent light bulb. Every time he was not successful—over the first 9,999 tries—he told himself he was that much closer to his solution.

Thomas Edison said that people who weren't successful didn't "realize how close they were to success when they gave up."

If you are working hard in some subject at school, don't give up. The more you try, even if you fail, the closer you become to success.

Fairness

A crucial character trait is fairness.

The dictionary says when a person is fair, that person is impartial, reasonable, and equitable. When you are impartial, you are not partial to anyone. You follow the rules, help others follow the rules, and do what is right.

A fair person wants the rules to work the same way for everyone. If you are fair, you don't try to take advantage of others. When you are playing a game and you are out, you need to admit you are out and not try to stay in the game. If you are playing a game and someone doesn't want to go out, remind that person that he or she is not being fair to everyone else. Fair means everyone has an equal chance at the game, following the same rules.

At _____ today, make sure you follow the rules in your classroom and on the playground. If you do, you make our school a wonderful place to be.

Learn from the Experience of Others

Plato

A long time ago a man named Plato said something interesting about talking to people older than you are. He said: "It gives me great pleasure to converse with the aged. They have been over the road that all of us must travel and know where it is rough and difficult and where it is level and easy."

People who are older have gone through similar experiences and can tell you what was difficult and what was easy for them. They can tell you what school was like and what their jobs were like. They can also tell you how you can avoid mistakes they have made. These can be people in your family or friends of your family who come to visit.

Don't be afraid to ask questions. By talking to people with more experience, you can learn a lot of important things that can help you.

Challenge/Failure/Success

George Clemenceau

*D*id you ever notice that even if you fail, you at least tried something?

The first time you try a sport or a new activity at school, don't be afraid that it is difficult or that you won't succeed perfectly.

A French leader during the time of World War I, George Clemenceau once said: "A man's life is interesting primarily when he had failed—for it's a sign that he tried to surpass himself."

If you don't try new things, you won't ever grow. Failure means you're trying something. Keep working at new things and you'll be more successful than people who would rather not try to do anything challenging at all.

Tenacity

Benjamin Zander

Benjamin Zander is the conductor of the Boston Philharmonic Orchestra. To be a conductor, you have to be a great musician. To be a great musician, you have to practice and not give up when you are tired or don't feel like practicing anymore. Benjamin Zander remembers taking cello lessons when he was eleven. His teacher, Mr. Herbert Withers, was eighty-three years old.

This is what Benjamin Zander remembers: "I had tried to play a passage, but I couldn't make it work. I tried again, and it didn't work, and a third time, and I was no more successful. I remember making a frustrated grimace and putting down my bow. The elderly Mr. Withers leaned over me and whispered, 'What? You've been practicing it for three minutes, and you still can't play it?'"

Benjamin Zander remembers his teacher was showing him not to expect to master anything, especially the playing of a musical passage, to be easy. It takes dedication and practice.

When you get to something difficult at school, remember that you have to be willing to practice and not give up when you are challenged.

New Ideas

Thomas Edison

Always be ready for someone to teach you something new. People who are curious discover new things every day.

Inventor Thomas Edison found solutions to problems and new ways to do things all the time. While working on things he would not give up because he would tell himself: "There is always a better way."

If you ever think you are the best at something be ready for someone to do the same thing differently. The fastest runner will have his or her record broken. The most popular video game, the biggest movie, and the most famous singer will eventually be replaced by someone or something new.

So today keep track of your new ideas. Your new idea can be the next thing to amaze the entire world because it is something completely new and different.

Learning

Clint Eastwood

No matter how old you are it is important to learn new things every day. It's very easy not to do anything—especially when you're not in school. Like any muscle, your brain needs regular exercise to stay fit. Actor, director, and former mayor of Carmel, California, Clint Eastwood said: "I'd like to be a bigger and more knowledgeable person ten years from now than I am today. I think that, for all of us, as we grow older, we must discipline ourselves to continue expanding, broadening, learning, keeping our minds active and open."

Keep a journal where you write down new ideas, stories, or questions you'd like to develop or study. Your life will be much more interesting if you keep your mind active with new ideas and continuous learning.

Be Good to Others

Abigail Van Buren

Are you good to everyone around you or are you only good to those who are similar to you? Some people are only good to their friends and mean to people they don't know or don't like.

Advice columnist Abigail Van Buren wrote: "The best index to a person's character is (a) how he treats people who can't do him any good, and (b) how he treats people who can't fight back."

The greatest people in the world are good to everyone—including those who are younger, smaller, older, and different from them. You never know who will be able to help you in the future. Some of these people who are different from you will do amazing things in the future. So today show you respect all people and are good to others because it is the right thing to do.

Respect Others

John W. De Forest

Respect has to do with how you look at things. The smaller parts of the word respect tell the story. RE means again and SPECT has to do with vision—which is where words like spectacles and spectacular come from. Every day you have opportunities to show how you look at others. If you respect them, you'll say positive, encouraging things. Don't let others lead you to show disrespect for others. Once you show disrespect for someone, it is hard to get that person to trust you again. Every little thing we do matters and shows whether we make good choices or bad choices.

John W. De Forest said: "It is not the great temptations that ruin us; it is the little ones."

Even a small show of disrespect to a friend or a teacher can ruin a relationship. So today make sure to be a positive example to others by showing you respect others by the way you talk to and about others.

Potential

Robert H. Schuller

*Y*ou can do amazing things. You be anything you want to be. Decide that you will try your hardest to be the best that you can be. Don't let chances to learn something new slide by without trying.

Robert H. Schuller once said: "There will never be another now—I will make the most of today. There will never be another me—I will make the most of myself."

Every day is a chance to expand your abilities. So today make the most of your time and your abilities. There will never be another today and there will never be another person exactly like you.

Change/Challenge

Robert Hooker

When you study something new, you are changing the way you think about something. In a way, you change who you are and what you know because you become smarter and understand things differently. In school you are expected to change and grow. Every week throughout your grade, your assignments become more difficult because it is your job to show growth. This means even as you become smarter, your studies will become more and more challenging. Expect some things to be difficult but don't tell yourself you cannot handle it. Be ready for the challenges and be confident that you can meet these challenges.

A British theologian named Robert Hooker once wrote: "Change is not made without inconvenience, even from worse to better."

This means you need to be ready for things to be difficult but don't give up. For things to become better and easier, you must first do the work. You have to get through the hard part for things to become easier. Then to keep growing you need to face the next challenge. So today be ready for the challenges that will be put in front of you. If things are very easy, be prepared because more difficult things are coming to challenge you.

Mastery of Learning Takes Time

John Champlin Gardner Jr.

$\mathcal{D}$id you know that a big storm gathers slowly over time? Thick, dark storm clouds come together to produce heavy rains, thunder, and lightning. One cloud cannot produce the same results all at once.

The man who wrote *Grendel* and other books, John Champlin Gardner Jr., wrote something about storms in connection with mastery of things you learn. He said: "Mastery is not something that strikes in an instant, like a thunderbolt, but a gathering power that moves steadily through time, like the weather."

Think of your everyday learning as a gathering storm. You aren't able to show you have mastered all your subject areas if you apply yourself for only one day or one week. Mastery of new information occurs over a long period of consistent effort.

So today remember to keep your efforts steady so that you will continue to grow and grow over time.

Kindness

Samuel Johnson

Have you ever given someone a nice surprise? It could have been something like a card or little gift or maybe it was a compliment to someone about something they do really well.

Have you ever received a nice surprise from someone? Maybe a friend gave you a small toy to take home or told you that you are a good friend. Sometimes small, nice, happy surprises can make us feel great.

Author Samuel Johnson lived in the 1700s and said this about what makes people happy: "Our brightest blazes of gladness are commonly kindled by unexpected sparks." This means that sometimes small, nice, happy surprises can make us feel great.

So today, try and make someone's day wonderful by surprising them with a happy, unexpected, kind word or deed. If you do, you will probably make their day surprisingly great.

Success/Trying

Henry David Thoreau

If you never try your best at something, you'll never know how much you can achieve. If you'd like to start playing tennis but have never gone onto a tennis court and tried hitting the ball back and forth with another person, you won't know how it feels or how much training you might need to become a great tennis player. Some people try new things and find out they are naturally talented in that particular area. You might be able to learn many languages or have a natural talent for cooking or you could be a really great baseball pitcher. You won't know if you don't try.

Once you start trying, then you need to put in the practice and not give up. One of America's greatest writers, Henry David Thoreau, said this about goals and trying hard at things: "We must walk consciously only part way toward our goal and then leap in the dark to our success."

Do you know you'll be successful at everything you try? No. But when you find something you'd like to try, give it the best effort you can and don't worry about not doing so well. The way to become a success is by trying your best and not giving up. If you're not a great success, by trying really hard you'll learn what you need to know to become successful the next time you try.

Potential

Orison Swett Marden

You can become anything you'd like to be. If you think of people you admire and respect, do you think they worked hard to become who they are? Do you wonder if it's possible for you to become that successful as well? If you want to be a president, doctor, teacher, actor, or anything else in this world, you need to recognize that you can do amazing things with your life. In a way you are the same as the people you admire. You are the same because you have the same twenty-four hours in a day they had when they were growing up and becoming more and more successful. You need to use your time in a similar way if you would like to be like them.

Orison Swett Marden wrote: "There are powers inside of you, which, if you could discover and use, would make of you everything you ever dreamed or imagined you could become."

You have the power to become anything you imagine. The power to become something great is inside of you. You just need to use your energy and your time to make your dream come true.

So today apply yourself in all the activities that you do because each day is an opportunity to improve your skills and get closer to becoming your dream.

Trying New Things

Henry Miller

When a baby begins to walk, the child does not recognize how many steps he or she will be able to take. They just try to walk and see how far they can get. It is spontaneous and without any prior experience.

As children get older, they recognize that doing something new for the first time can be scary. If you've never tried something, there is a chance that you'll fail. If you never try something new, you'll never grow.

Author Henry Miller wrote: "All growth is a leap in the dark, a spontaneous, unpremeditated act without benefit of experience."

Don't hesitate to try new things. Get all the experience you can. People who avoid new things are those that do not grow. Today think of new things you will try and do. If you don't keep a journal or diary, start keeping notes on the things you'd like to try because new experiences lead to growth.

Challenge/Worthwhile Work

Margaret Thatcher

Happiness comes from doing things you enjoy. If you think about your most satisfying days, they are usually days where you've done lots of things. This has to do with challenging yourself to do great things. On a busy day you might doubt you can finish everything that needs to be done—that's part of the challenge and excitement of that sort of day.

Margaret Thatcher said: "Look at a day when you are supremely satisfied at the end. It's not a day when you lounge around doing nothing; it's when you've everything to do, and you've done it."

So today think of all you need to get done and look forward to the challenge. If you do worthwhile things throughout the day you will feel a greater sense of accomplishment than if you do not challenge yourself.

Failure Is a Prerequisite to Success

Theodore Roosevelt

People who refuse to try new things never experience great successes. If you don't dare to dream of great things and attempt them, you'll never have amazing experiences. People who stick with what they know do this to avoid ever feeling great failure.

Theodore Roosevelt once said: "Far better to dare mighty things, to win glorious triumphs, even though checkered by failure, than to take rank with those poor spirits who neither enjoy much nor suffer much, because they live in the gray twilight that knows not victory, nor defeat."

Don't be afraid of not being successful. Failure is required if you are to be successful. If you try doing your best on assignments, don't be afraid of what corrections you might need to make. Learn from the feedback your teachers give you and use it to improve. Today make sure to try doing the best you've ever done on difficult assignments, even if you might not be successful. If you do this, you're on your way to experiencing great successes in the future.

Kindness

Ralph Waldo Emerson

Being kind to others is good for your health. Your brain and your heart function best when there is a feeling that something good is happening. When you feel good your body releases chemicals called endorphins that make you better able to learn. It is also important to help others because you won't always see the same people every day of your life. There are times when people move away and all of a sudden we don't have the chance to be nice to them anymore.

Ralph Waldo Emerson wrote: "You cannot do a kindness too soon, for you never know how soon it will be too late."

So today take the time to be kind to someone else. You'll feel good about yourself and you'll make that person's day happier as well.

Improvement

Rene Descartes

If you receive a low grade on a report card, don't feel like you cannot do anything about it. Tell yourself you just need to get started doing something differently in the area where you need to improve. What you were doing before was unsuccessful so now you need to decide what you need to do differently to change the results. Don't think it's too late or you're too far behind. Start little by little mastering the parts of the area where you need improvement. If you're weak in multiplication, start making flash cards of the facts you haven't memorized. If you are weak in social studies, read over the chapter you're struggling with a few times and review the material with a friend or your family.

Rene Descartes thought it was important to divide a big difficulty into smaller parts. He said: "Divide each difficulty into as many parts as necessary to resolve it."

With any problem or area of study, divide what you need to do into smaller parts. The key is to get started on those little steps. Once you start doing something about the problem, you'll be on your way to better results.

Positive Thinking/Results

James Allen

Your thoughts influence what you say and do. If you think that working hard is important, you'll enjoy finishing your work and you'll look forward to starting the next project. This type of positive thinking will lead you to be successful.

Author James Allen said: "Work joyfully and peacefully, knowing that the right thoughts and right efforts will inevitably bring about right results."

In the end if you want positive results you need to do positive things. If you want to get good grades, think about your assignments as helpful and necessary. If you think your assignments are a waste of time, you will never really enjoy your classes and you will end up being less successful. Instead, train your mind to think positively since your thoughts guide your choices and lead you to the results you deserve.

Friendship

Ralph Waldo Emerson

How do you make and keep friends? Treat others in a fair, friendly, caring way. Be honest with them. Be helpful. Show through your actions that you think their thoughts are important.

Ralph Waldo Emerson said something extremely important about having friends. He said: "The only reward of virtue is virtue; the only way to have a friend is to be one."

So today show you know how to have great friends. Make sure your friends know they are important to you by the way you treat them.

Choices/Truth

Marcus Aurelius

Marcus Aurelius, who was a Roman emperor and philosopher, lived from 121–180. He believed people should be responsible. Marcus Aurelius thought people should think before choosing to say or do something.

He said: "If it is not right, do not do it; if it is not true, do not say it."

Marcus Aurelius was right. Be a model for others in everything you say and do. By making good choices you make the world a better place.

Goal Setting/Hard Work

John F. Kennedy

Why did people create helicopters, planes, and rockets? Someone had to first have an idea that they were excited about. Someone had the vision that space flight was possible and over time lots of different men and women had to conduct experiments to figure out how a large machine could go up in the air like a bird. Was this something simple? Not at all.

In fact, President John F. Kennedy in 1962 said: "We choose to go to the moon. We choose to go to the moon in this decade and do the other things, not because they are easy, but because they are hard."

Doing difficult things brings great rewards. If you do easy things all the time, you don't feel a sense of accomplishment because you already knew you could do these simple things. If you get a difficult thing done, you feel better about yourself since you stretched your abilities further. Space flight is a great example of how people can do amazing things if they set their minds to a great goal and work on it with all their might.

Do the Impossible

Arthur Clarke

Grete Waitz was twenty-five years old in 1978. She had never run a marathon before. She didn't even know anyone who had ever run a long distance. But since she was a member of the Norwegian national track team who was used to running short races, she decided to enter the New York City Marathon. She did the best she could and she ended up setting a world record by running 26.2 miles in two hours, thirty-two minutes, thirty seconds. She did what was not yet possible at that time.

The great author of *2001: A Space Odyssey*, Arthur Clarke, who thought about the future in terms of what would be possible, wrote: "The only way to discover the limits of the possible is to go beyond them into the impossible."

Try your best at everything you do. If someone tells you that it's impossible or that no one has ever done what you are trying to do, remember that you can be the first to do something no one else thought was possible.

Success/Failure

Herman Melville

Can you be great at everything you'd like to do the very first time you do it? Everyone must learn to do things and refine their skills as they grow. To do things perfectly the first time would be incredibly rare.

This means it is only logical that people need to fail and make mistakes before they are great at something.

The author of such great books as *Moby Dick* and *Billy Budd*, Herman Melville, wrote: "He who has never failed somewhere, that man cannot be great."

So today make sure to try your best at all you are working on. Don't worry about failure. Encourage others when they are unsuccessful because they are getting closer to becoming great at something. Failure leads to success.

Choices/Contribution

John Keats

How can you do some good for the world? Everyone can take the time to help someone else every day. You can do this at school through the way you interact with other students and with adults. Your actions should reflect your good intentions. Make contributions to your class by participating and getting your work done. Help those who need help. Follow the rules and compliment others who demonstrate great skill.

John Keats wrote: "I find that there is no worthy pursuit but the idea of doing some good to the world."

So today find ways to show you are doing some good in the world through the choices you make.

SPECIAL DAYS

September 11

On September 11, 2001, many people in New York City around where the Twin Tower buildings stood and at the Pentagon building in the Washington, D.C., area showed the meaning of courage. The extraordinary bravery shown by firefighters, police, medical teams, brave citizens, and others saved thousands of lives. These people ran toward danger to keep others safe.

These men and women put themselves at risk, as they do every day, to do what was right—to help others. On September 11th these people did more than their job or any job requires. In New York City, 353 brave men died that day while doing their jobs. Until then, no fire had taken the lives of more than twelve firefighters at one time. A note left on a firehouse shrine spoke for many by saying, YOU RAN IN WHEN WE RAN OUT, WE ARE GRATEFUL FOREVER.

There are no greater heroes than those who serve others. So today, think about how important it is to help others and what you can do to show that you are a good citizen.

Veteran's Day

A veteran is someone who has served in the U.S. armed forces. Veteran's Day is an annual holiday set aside to honor those men and women who have served our country. You may know someone who has served in the army, air force, marines, navy, or in some other special way.

Take a moment to thank that person for the good things they have done for our country. Find out where they served and tell them you appreciate how they left their homes and families for a time to do something our country asked them to do.

Thanksgiving

Thanksgiving is a time to show appreciation for the good things we have.

Take the time to share with your family what you are thankful for. It could be your home, the people you live with, or it could be the way that others help you when you need help. Sometimes too many opportunities pass by when we could have said kind things to others. Don't let this special holiday go by without thinking about what is good in your life and sharing it with someone else.

Since you won't be in class on Thanksgiving, take a moment today to tell your teacher how thankful you are for the way you are taught at _____ .

Winter Break

In eastern Tibet it is common for people to greet one another with the words *Tashi deley*.

It means "I honor the greatness in you. I honor the place in you where lives your courage, honor, love, hope, and dreams."

During this winter break take the time to acknowledge the greatness in others. Every person has hope, dreams, love, honor, and courage in them.

Take the time to think about your own hopes and dreams. Use this time off to enjoy yourself and to think about what is important to you. The word re-creation literally means to "re-create" yourself so you can go back to work with more energy and more focus than you had before.

I honor the greatness in you. I honor the place in you where lives your courage, honor, love, hope, and dreams. *Tashi deley*.

Presidents' Day/John. F. Kennedy

*D*id you know that you can become president even if you have health problems or some type of condition that requires you to receive extra help?

President John F. Kennedy is an example of this. When he was a child he had scarlet fever, jaundice, and measles. As an adult he had back problems that caused him great pain. He had a form of Addison's disease. Kennedy used to see doctors regularly, stayed in the hospital many times, and had several surgeries.

Even though he had several challenging illnesses, he became our country's thirty-fifth president.

So remember, even if you have a special condition, don't let it stop you from setting a goal of doing something amazing. You can become whatever it is you want to be.

Presidents' Day/George Washington

What was George Washington's favorite subject? Math. He was so good in math that he decided to become a surveyor. A surveyor is someone who measures land. You have probably seen many pictures of him using what look like binoculars to look around a piece of land. He would then write down measurements so people could keep track of the size and type of land that was in the area. He later joined the army, became our first president, and used his skills to make many important decisions about our country.

When you think about your skills, think about using them in ways that help others. If there is a way to help in the classroom, volunteer to help. Become someone who is known for being helpful and you will make the world a better place.

St. Patrick's Day

Saint Patrick's Day is celebrated each year on March 17. The festive holiday has everyone wearing green (so they don't get pinched) and chatting of four leaf clovers, shamrocks, lucky leprechauns, and kissing some big rock called a Blarney stone. Does it all sound a bit strange? It did to me too but after a bit of research it all made sense. Here's what I found out. Did you know that Saint Patrick's name at birth was Maewyn Succat? He was born in Wales somewhere near the end of the fourth century and took on the name Patrick or Patricus, after he became a priest, much later in his life. He was known for helping Irish people become Christians.

Patrick's mission in Ireland lasted for thirty years. He then retired to County Down and died on March 17 in 461 A.D. That day has been commemorated as St. Patrick's Day ever since. The first year St. Patrick's Day was celebrated in this country was 1737 in Boston, Massachusetts. Here are some terms you might hear connected to St. Patrick's Day:

Shamrock: St. Patrick used the shamrock leaf with it's three leaves while teaching. Today many people wear a shamrock to commemorate Saint Patrick's Day. It is considered lucky to find a rare four leaf clover on St. Patrick's Day.

Blarney Stone: So what's all this talk of kissing the Blarney stone? Blarney Castle is located in County Cork, Ireland. Built in 1446 by Cormac Laidhim McCarthy (Lord of Muskerry) the Blarney stone is located in the southern tower wall between the main castle wall and the parapet. In order to kiss the stone one has to lie on their back and bend backward (and downward), holding iron bars for support. It is said that the Blarney stone has magical properties. As legend has it an old woman cast a spell on the stone to reward a king who had saved her from drowning. Kissing the stone gave the king the ability to speak sweetly and convincingly.

Leprechaun: Just what does a Leprechaun look like and why are they so special? A Leprechaun (Irish fairy) looks like a little old man. He's about two feet tall and dresses like a shoemaker with a hat and leather apron. A Leprechaun's personality is described as aloof and unfriendly. They live alone and pass the time by making shoes. They're special because they also possess a hidden pot of gold.

Green: Green is the color of spring, shamrocks, and is connected with hope and nature.

Secretary's Day/Administrative Professionals Day

$\mathcal{T}$oday is Secretary's Day. On some calendars it is known as Administrative Professionals Day. This day is a day we should express our thanks to those who work in the front office. They are the ones who answer questions and help parents, teachers, and students all day long. They care for students who become ill or have an emergency, they assist families new to our area when they need to start attending our school, and they help process all the materials we need for the projects we do at school. There are really so many things they do all day that it is impossible to name them all. But today, please make sure to say thank you to them when you see them in the office. They are very important to _____ .

Space Day

About 2,400 years ago, a philosopher named Socrates lived in Greece. He was famous for teaching others. He enjoyed thinking about what people know and how they learn.

He said something interesting about how we can really learn about the world: "Man must rise above the earth—to the top of the atmosphere and beyond—for only thus will he fully understand the world in which he lives."

Thousands of years before the first flight took place, Socrates was talking about going above the earth to understand it better. We live at a time when flying through space on a plane or in a helicopter is common. Watching the news to see pictures from outer space is exciting to us but not a surprise because humans have invented ways to travel through space and get information we can use about how things live on Earth and away from Earth. All of these flying machines are used to help people see things they wouldn't be able to see otherwise.

Socrates probably didn't know all the ways we'd be able to travel but I'm sure he'd be very impressed to know that his thoughts about rising above the earth thousands of years ago have come true.

Mother's Day

Abraham Lincoln

This Sunday take a moment to honor your mother. From the time you were conceived to today, others had to look after you. You needed to be cared for, fed, taught, and appreciated in order to grow. Think of how often your mother had to do things for you while you were growing up. Her voice, her ideas, and her gifts to you helped make you the person you are today.

Regarding his mother, Abraham Lincoln said: "Everything I am or ever hope to be, I owe to my angel mother."

We each owe a great deal to our mothers or any other women who may help take care of us. If in your family there are other women who positively influenced your development, take a moment to thank them as well. This might include a grandmother, stepmother, or an aunt. One of the greatest gifts you can give is showing love and appreciation. This Mother's Day, make a special effort to tell your mother how much she has contributed to your success.

Memorial Day

As we get ready to celebrate Memorial Day it is important to note that this day should be used to remember men and women who have passed away while defending our country. These people were asked to go away from their homes and families to do something important. They may have served in the army, navy, marines, air force, or in some other special way. These people did not return home safely to their families and deserve to be remembered.

The word memorial comes from the same root word as the word memory, so think of Memorial Day as a memory day. On Memorial Day take a moment to remember these important people who passed away.

Father's Day

Every year a special day is dedicated to fathers. Have you already thought of something special you'll do this year for your father?

An English proverb from the seventeenth century stated: "One father is more than a hundred schoolmasters."

Fathers teach us ideals and principles that guide our thoughts and decisions. They provide for their families by caring for their needs.

When making a special day for someone so important in your life, think of what that person enjoys doing. Do something he enjoys. Think ahead and plan a few surprises. It could be fun to create a small list of all the great things you can do for him throughout the day. If you haven't written a special card or letter, start working on it so it's something he'll always remember.

Fathers do amazing things for their children. They deserve our appreciation. Take this opportunity to remind your father how special he is to you.

Subject Index

actions/choices, 66
age is irrelevant/success at any age, 115
anger management, 79, 87
attitude/positive thoughts, 70

be positive, 76
be good to others, 127
brain/depression, 112
brain/healthy eating, 74
brain/positive messages, 114
brain/rest/learning, 91

caring, 52
challenges/confidence, 29
challenge/failure/success, 98, 123
challenge/worthwhile work, 136
change/challenge, 130
choices, 103
choices/actions, 72
choices/actions reflect character, 9
choices/anger, 96
choices/contribution, 146
choices/truth, 142
choose your attitude, 64
citizenship, 17
confidence, 37
constant improvement, 110

do extra/read and study more, 118
do more than you are required, 73
do the impossible, 144

effort, 78
emotional energy, 6
energy, 63
environment, 19
excellence/hard work, 39
exercise, 12, 48, 58

failure/success, 89
failure is a prerequisite to success, 137
fairness, 121
family/show appreciation, 105
fears/confidence, 31
focus, 117
friendship, 141

habits/tenacity, 3

goal setting, 8, 67, 69, 88, 100
goal setting/hard work, 143
goal setting/obstacles, 35

hard work/success, 108
health/drinking water, 30

Subject Index

health/drinking milk, 116
healthy habits, 38
helping others, 7

improvement, 15, 139
individual greatness, 82
inner beauty/judgment, 93
intentions, 41

kindness, 132, 138
knowledge/goal setting, 106

learn from experience of others, 122
learn from mistakes, 75
learning, 10, 81, 84, 126
learning/curiosity, 101
listening, 4

make a difference, 33
making mistakes, 68
mastery of learning takes time, 131
mistakes/success/failure, 94

new ideas, 34, 125

opportunities, 16
opportunities/choices, 20
opportunity, 119

persistence, 50, 53
positive influences, 21
positive thinking, 23, 26, 43, 107
positive thinking/results, 140
positive thoughts, 80, 99
positive thoughts/contribution, 104
potential, 62, 129, 134
practice, 13
problem solving, 18, 47
problem solving/responsibility, 61

quality, 113

reading, 22, 27, 102, 109
reading/learning, 85
respect others, 128
responsibility/choices, 56

self-control/paying attention, 57
self-control/thoughts, 45
show appreciation, 32
success/failure, 60, 145
success/tenacity, 25
success/trying, 133

talents, 14
talents/boldness, 24
teaching others, 65
tenacity, 2, 28, 77, 83, 95, 97, 120, 124
tenacity/success, 111
think before you act, 1
thinking/dreaming, 86
thoughts/dreams/goals, 42
time management, 71
time management/listening, 40
tolerance, 44
tolerance/respect for others, 46
trustworthiness, 51, 59, 90
truth, 55
try new things, 11, 135

vision, 92

water/brain, 54
work habits, 49
work hard, 36

your speech reflects your character, 5

Author Index

Aaron, Hank, 50
Adair, Margo, 114
Adams, Charles Kendall, 73
Addams, Jane, 52
Aesop, 3
Alan of Lille, 26
Allen, James, 140
Arie de Geus, 84
Aristides, 5
Armstrong, Lance, 21
Ashe, Liz, 15
Aurelius, Marcus, 142

Barrett, Colleen C., 70
Beecher, Henry Ward, 97
Bell, Alexander Graham, 88, 105
Benn, Alonzo Newton, 29
Bronte, Anne, 13
Buck, Pearl, 39
Buxton, Sir Thomas Fowell, 33

Chinese proverbs, 27, 61
Clarke, Arthur, 144
Clemenceau, George, 123
Crane, Frank, 80

De Forest, John W., 128
Descartes, Rene, 22, 139

Eastwood, Clint, 126
Edison, Thomas, 111, 120, 125
Edwards, Robert C., 41
Einstein, Albert, 94
Eisenhower, Dwight D., 78
Eliot, George, 9, 115
Emerson, Ralph Waldo, 7, 16, 45, 138, 141

Forbes, B. C., 60
Ford, Henry, 18, 75
Frankl, Viktor, 64

Gandhi, Mahatma, 104
Gardner, John Champlin, Jr., 131
Glasow, Arnold H., 23
Greenlaw, Linda, 106

Hale, Edward E., 17
Hamilton, Jane, 85
Hemingway, Ernest, 4
Herold, Don, 101
Hilton, Conrad, 2
Hooker, Robert, 130
Hugo, Victor, 47
Huxley, Aldous, 55
Huxley, Thomas Henry, 25

Irving, Washington, 8

Author Index

Jackson, Reggie, 89
Johnson, Samuel, 132
Jones, Charlie, 109
Jordan, Michael, 83

Keats, John, 146
Kennedy, John F., 143
King, Martin Luther, Jr., 103
Korda, Michael, 42
Krone, Julieanne Louise, 67
Kubler-Ross, Elisabeth, 56

Lao-tzu, 96
Lincoln, Abraham, 77, 79

Marden, Orison Swett, 134
Marshall, Peter, 20
Maslow, Abraham, 81
Matsoff, Angie, 28
McKay, James T., 62
Melville, Herman, 145
Michelangelo, 93
Miller, Henry, 135

Newton, Howard, 113

O'Connor, Sandra Day, 19

Pareto, Vilfredo, 71
Plato, 122
Powell, Colin, 98

Riley, Samantha, 100
Rohn, Jim, 102
Roosevelt, Eleanor, 31
Roosevelt, Theodore, 37, 108, 137
Ruskin, John, 66

Sagan, Carl, 10
Schuller, Robert H., 129
Smith, Sydney, 35
Sophocles, 36
Steel, Janeen, 95

Thatcher, Margaret, 136
Thayer, Nancy, 110
Thoreau, Henry David, 51, 133
Tracy, Brian, 69
Twain, Mark, 112

Van Buren, Abigail, 127
Van Gogh, Vincent, 1, 11, 86
Vietnamese proverb, 32
Vonnegut, Kurt, 107

Waitz, Grete, 144
Watson, Thomas, 34
Weinbaum, Dave, 119
Wilson, Oliver G., 14
Wolfe, Thomas, 24

Zander, Benjamin, 124

About the Author

Edward P. Fiszer received a doctorate of education in educational leadership from UCLA. He is a school principal, enjoys teaching graduate courses in educational leadership, and is the author of *How Teachers Learn Best: An Ongoing Professional Development Model* (ScarecrowEducation, 2003).